OTHER
PEOPLE'S
MONEY

ECONOMIC
ESSAYS

*Other
People's
Money*

H. C. Coombs

AUSTRALIAN NATIONAL UNIVERSITY PRESS
CANBERRA 1971

Printed and manufactured in Australia by Gillingham Printers Pty Ltd
Adelaide.
Registered in Australia for trans-
mission by post as a book.
National Library of Australia Card
no. and ISBN—
0   7081   0126   7   (clothbound)
0   7081   0128   3   (paperbound)
Library of Congress Catalog Card
no. 75–153051.

PREFACE

T HESE essays represent a selection of addresses and papers presented or published from 1949 to 1968 during my term as Governor of the Commonwealth Bank of Australia and subsequently of the Reserve Bank of Australia. They represent, I think, a fair record of the changing patterns of thought underlying central banking policies during that time. Looking back over them I am struck by the changing emphasis in the theoretical concepts influencing economic analyses within the Bank and the degree to which it was necessary finally to rely on intuitive judgment about the factors at work within the economy and financial system. As I remarked in the Giblin Lecture, we seem in retrospect to have always been forced to make the bricks of decision while struggling to gather the straw of understanding.

It may perhaps be of interest to describe the procedure followed in the preparation of most of these papers. It was the practice in the Bank to have almost daily informal consultations among senior officers of policy departments and weekly meetings of a formally established Central Banking Advisory Committee to both of which younger officers from research and operational departments were from time to time invited. When an address or paper was proposed—sometimes as the result of an invitation but often at our own initiative—I would discuss with one or both of these groups the proposed subject and the broad lines on which it might be dealt with. A younger officer would then be commissioned to prepare a draft for discussion by the group and thereafter to redraft it in the light of the discussion. The purpose of these discussions was to clarify the issues, to sharpen our individual understanding of them, and to expose the policy alternatives. They were not designed to produce a consensus.

Finally I would rewrite the paper myself, expressing my own views as they had developed in the light of the discussion. Generally the final document bore little apparent relationship to the drafts, and both content and words were my personal responsibility. Nevertheless, the views and judgments expressed were in large measure forged in the fire of argument, and therefore in significant ways they represent the outcome of the corporate process which led to their composition. The function of the early drafts was to act as a kind of catalyst in this process.

I am indebted therefore to my colleagues in an intimate and complex way for their help in the composition of the papers, and it is difficult to single out individuals for special mention. However, I would like to record my special thanks to those officers who worked on the early drafting and who may at times have felt that their labours had borne little fruit. I hope, if they look back over the collection, they will see the papers as the product of team work to which their personal contribution was critical.

Finally I should like to thank Professor H. W. Arndt, who has selected and edited the papers. He has, as always, been percipient, patient, and conscientious.

Sydney 1970   H. C. C.

CONTENTS

BANKERS,
MOUNTEBANKS,
AND SCHOLARS

BANKERS have an unenviable reputation for hardness of heart, closeness of emotional attitudes and orthodoxy in their financial and political views. Such appellations as 'the hard-faced men of Martin Place' suggest that they are not regarded as the friendliest of souls.

However, caution and orthodoxy have not always been characteristic of bankers. Indeed, like many others equally respectable, the family is obscure in origin and seems to contain a substantial degree of brigandage in its early generations. I should think many bankers today read with a certain nostalgia the story of the rapid and spectacular rise of John Law, an obscure Scottish student who took advantage of the financial difficulties of the King of France to persuade His Majesty to allow him to found the Royal Bank. Law was the first student of monetary theory fully to seize upon the advantages of bank notes being legal tender. He persuaded the King to decree that the notes of the Bank were to be accepted in payment of taxes. Since the coinage of the day was of uncertain value—being depreciated not by the subtle modern method of inflation but by the cruder confiscations of clippers, sweaters and counterfeiters—notes which had guaranteed value became instantly popular. People rushed to invest in the Bank and to entrust their savings to it. Law went from strength to strength. He took over the whole of the National debt and was in the process of buying out one of the great overseas trading companies of the era.

At this stage he made a tragic blunder. He was, like all innovators, subject to some criticism and, stung by this and blinded by the Scotsman's faith in reason and argument, he published certain pamphlets in defence of his theories. The effect was apparently devastating—faith in his Bank dispersed like mist in the wind and before long it had failed and John Law had fled the country. Since then bankers have come to realise that the only literature they should ever publish is that bearing the words 'Legal tender for the sum of . . .' or, if this procedure cannot safely be evaded, the words 'Received from . . . the sum of £ . . .'

Sydney University Union Visitors' Annual Dinner, 28 July 1959.

Indeed, this taciturnity has become so characteristic of the profession that Mr John T. Lang, a deep student of these matters, claims that the bankers' motto is 'Never explain—never justify'.

Certainly, one could well believe this from an acquaintance with the life and work of Montagu Norman, the last great mystery man of High Finance. With his pointed beard and his wide brimmed black hat he was a spectacular figure and many people were sceptical as to whether his practice of dashing from international capital to international capital —appearing in the passenger lists as Professor Skinner—was designed to conceal or advertise his movements. Similarly, his gift for wrapping his every move in an enigmatic aura of silence roused the profoundest admiration and suspicion.

There can be no doubt of his ability. He was the first Governor of the Bank of England to hold that office for more than a year or two. He built that institution into an integral unit of the machinery of govern-ment of the United Kingdom, which has survived through political and social change of near revolutionary extent. He was responsible too for the creation of an international freemasonary of central bankers that cuts across barriers of nationality, race, and creed. Yet, if a first-year student of monetary theory were to base his answers on the evidence of Mr Norman, say before the McMillan Committee, he would almost certainly be failed.

Silence too was a characteristic of Arthur Alvis Rees, a man who forced his way into the magic circle of bankers by private enterprise of a highly individual character. He had long wanted to be a banker— not just a clerk or a teller, a manager, a governor or other such under-ling, but one who *owned* a bank—a Morgan or a Rothschild. Like many of us he lacked the capital to fulfil this ambition but unlike most of us he was undeterred by this handicap.

Armed with some counterfeit official letterheads from the Bank of Portugal, some natural aptitude in penmanship, and the aid of a friend in the diplomatic service, he persuaded one of the greatest note printing firms in the world to accept as official an order for the equivalent of more than £Stg 1m. worth of Portuguese currency. In due course he took delivery and with the capital provided by the currency he set up a new bank through which he then distributed the notes by making loans and investments. It was an enterprising bank and put its more conservative fellows to shame.

In due course the forgeries were detected and ultimately the enter-prising Mr Rees was convicted and sentenced—but not before he and his confrères had gone within striking distance of acquiring sufficient shares to give a controlling interest over the Bank of Portugal itself— a central bank which was at that time still privately owned—and not before he had produced forged documents which purported to involve the Governor of the Bank himself in this gigantic swindle. These documents led to the arrest and imprisonment of the Governor of the Bank, although he was soon exonerated. There was an interesting tail piece to this story—the counsel for the accused argued that at the time the economy was in need of an expansionist monetary policy and that so far from doing any harm they had helped maintain the economy and furthermore the notes were not counterfeit but genuine, although duplicates, and that they had been paid for—an ingenious defence but Rees was sentenced to twenty years' imprisonment.

These examples may serve to demonstrate that even bankers are human—but then banking is an intensely human occupation. Every bank account is a record of a man's hopes and ambitions—his struggles, achievements, and failures—and every loan is a gamble on the quality and character of the borrower. However, as one gets away from the direct contact with the individual customer, the consciousness of this human element is more difficult to keep fresh and vigorous—and a central banker is isolated from those who are affected by his decisions by many intermediaries. There are dangers in this isolation and consequently it has seemed to me wise that a banker should try to renew his humanity by activity in other fields.

For my part I have turned to theatre and to universities. They may seem an odd combination but they have interesting similarities as well as differences. Certainly taciturnity has no place in their lives—from both pours forth an apparently unending stream of words spoken and written. They share a tendency to produce 'prima donnas' and a passionate conviction of the ultimate value of their own work. This latter produces a fine contempt for financial limitations. I am amused from time to time at finding myself caught up in this enthusiasm and arguing to those who hold the various purse-strings that whatever else goes short it clearly should not be theatre—or university, as the case may be.

I like the theatre—it is a warm and living thing. In an age when the arts have become alienated from humanity—when our painters paint merely paint and our musicians compose organised noises—it is good that there is an art which is wholly and unashamedly devoted to mankind. In an age when we are urged to enjoy even our vicarious experience filtered through the shadows of screen and television set there remains the theatre where the performance is an experience shared and where communication is a living thing.

Above all, I like theatre because I believe Australians have a natural gift for it—not merely do we produce actors, singers, dancers, performers of all sorts for the world but we have the raw material for genuine creation. There is in the Australian character and temperament a streak of violence, a gift for colourful and rhythmic speech, a salty, deflating scepticism, which combine to give force, content, and individuality to dramatic work.

It is less than five years since the Elizabethan Theatre Trust began to give an outlet for Australian creative effort in the theatre. Since then we have had *The Doll*, *The Shifting Heart*, *The Slaughter*, and *The Bastard Country*, four plays through which is scattered with lavish hand the proof of capacity. There is too *Dalgerie*—an operatic fragment of profoundly moving quality, produced by the Trust in Perth last year. These are the works of the Beaumonts and Fletchers of our dramatic age. Within the next decade I am certain Australia will produce great drama. To be in Australian theatre today, even as an onlooker as I am, is to be aware of vitality and growth as abounding as a ferment of yeast. Who will write these plays? Perhaps Ray Lawler—but not if he remains an expatriate, pursuing the phantom of tax avoidance—perhaps one of the authors whose work has already been tried—perhaps Ray Mathew—a poet and dramatist of sensitivity and power whose best work has yet to be done.

'In the long run', said J. M. Keynes, 'we'll all be dead' and in the field of economic and monetary policy our range of vision does not seek to peer far into the future. We live from hand to mouth or at least from wool clip to wool clip and if we can pass into the next stage of planning with stability and growth maintained and our economic defences reasonable, we heave a sigh of relief and advance our sights a cautious year or two.

As a counter to this myopic concentration, it is good for a banker to turn to universities. Here he will meet strange characters—prima donnas of learning—men with a burning passion for truth within the narrow confines of their own walnut of knowledge but often as blind with prejudice and unreason outside this as the most unlearned of mortals. He will find some who have the artists' conviction that their personal hopes and disappointments are matters of universal significance. He will see work being done the value of which he cannot hope to conceive.

Gradually, however, he will come to realise that these people form part of a community which extends beyond and across the national and racial barriers of the world—which extends through time from the Ancient Greeks through the present and far into the future. He will see that when their work is looked at in perspective, it pushes back by steady labour and by brilliant erratic leaps of intuition the darkness of ignorance. He will see that the very eccentricity and extravagance of some is a means of preserving the sources of insight, the freedom of inquiry, and the right to hold heterodox opinions which are in my view the foundations of civilisation.

These freedoms have not been easily won—nor are they ever won for all time. They are threatened and must be fought for in every generation. It is the especial obligation of those who have been privileged to live and work in universities to help protect these rights after they have taken their places in the world. The need for this is great today when competing certainties seek to impose their ways of thought upon the world. I trust that you will accept this obligation.

PART I

---

*Banking and
Monetary Policy*

The Development
of Monetary
Policy in Australia

THERE has been in recent years a change in the attitude towards monetary policy. Most of us can remember when anything which had anything to do with money was both in the mediaeval and modern sense of the term something of a mystery; an activity carried on by an exclusive group behind closed doors.

In these times almost anybody is prepared to express views on monetary and banking policy—some of them less well-informed than they might be. Although those responsible for monetary policy act in the light of the fullest knowledge available, and I believe with a high sense of responsibility, it is important that monetary as well as other economic problems should be the subject of analysis and discussion.

The mystery element in monetary policy was sharply reduced with the emergence of what has been described as the 'Keynesian Revolution' in economics. The Keynesian analysis of the economic system provided the means by which the effects of monetary policy could be assessed. The essence of the Keynesian analysis was that in a market economy the level of production and employment is determined by the level of spending; spending by households, by firms and businesses, and by public authorities and government. And consequently it followed that there is a level of spending which is sufficient to employ the whole of the labour and available resources of the economy. If spending falls short of that level the economy will experience unemployment and resources will be idle. On the other hand, if spending exceeds that level, since output and employment can be increased no further, the increased spending will show itself in rising prices and shortages of goods, labour, and materials.

This over-simplified version of the Keynesian analysis brings out the significance of spending on employment and production and thereby provides us with a criterion by which monetary policy can be tested. What will be the effect of a given policy on spending? Would such an

The English, Scottish and Australian Bank Research Lecture, University of Queensland, 15 September 1954. Reproduced by permission of the University of Queensland Press.

effect be appropriate in the current condition of employment and production?

Any given piece of expenditure can be financed from one of four sources (or a combination of these sources):

(1) new savings;

(2) accumulated reserves;

(3) money borrowed, other than from a bank;

(4) money borrowed from a bank.

The last source differs from the first three because when money is lent by a bank it passes into the hands of the person who borrows it without anybody having less. Whenever a bank lends money there is, therefore, an increase in the total amount of money available.

Spending can be influenced by the amount of money which is available in a community and also by the freedom with which people will draw upon their stocks of money to spend or lend. It can be influenced also by the willingness of banks to lend. Since monetary policy can influence both the supply of money and the willingness of banks to lend, and consequently the total volume of spending, there is a close connection between the monetary policy and levels of employment and production. Monetary policy can be examined, either in prospect or retrospect, by tracing its effects on spending, production, and employment and judging whether these effects are appropriate to current circumstances.

Monetary policy is not good or bad in itself. Almost any form of monetary action can be justified in some circumstances and can be utterly wrong in others. For instance, I can remember when people used to get very agitated about a central bank lending to its government. Such loans, like any other form of monetary action, are good or bad according to the circumstances in which they are made. We must beware of an approach to monetary policy in terms of rigid rules. The test of monetary policy is in its effects.

With these things in mind we can turn to the development of monetary policy in Australia over the last few decades. It is an interesting thing that the first result of the emergence of the Keynesian analysis was rather to push monetary policy as such into the background. For a while it came to be regarded as purely incidental to public expenditure policy and consequently as having little initiative of itself. This tendency arose largely from the conviction that grew out of the depression of the 1930s, that there was an inherent tendency in a market economy for expenditure to be insufficient to sustain employment and production. If this conviction were true, monetary policy became simply the means to increase expenditure—a task in which the initiative needed should properly be with governments, businesses, and individuals; the banking system acting as the responsive servant of governments and of industry to provide finance as called upon. In a period of substantial under-employment of resources this was perhaps not an unreasonable over-simplification. It was clear that almost anything which increased the level of expenditure would overall have desirable effects. In such a situation monetary policy inevitably came to be looked on as a secondary and rather passive instrument of economic policy.

The war pushed monetary policy even further into the background. The economic problem of the war was to divert the physical and human resources of the economy to the greatest possible extent to activities associated with the war. Such a diversion, once resources were fully employed, required the withdrawal of resources away from other activities. In a financial sense these two aspects of wartime policy were reflected in tremendous expenditure by government, and by measures to restrict expenditure by all other persons, firms and authorities which might require the production of goods not strictly necessary for war purposes. The government's military expenditure was financed from the proceeds of taxes and public loans but also by borrowing from the Central Bank. Measures to restrict other expenditure included taxation and loan raising but also a variety of more direct limitations. By rationing and by various forms of control people were prevented from spending. Furthermore, price control was imposed on the whole range of goods available so that the amount of money which could be spent on civil goods was limited. As a result people and businesses found they earned far more money than they could spend even after taxes, and there was steadily built up a large accumulation of deposits in the banks and of notes in the hands of the public. By the end of the war, the volume of money was 120 per cent higher than it had been at the outbreak of the war. Thus throughout the war the role of the monetary authority was the largely passive one of providing the financial needs of government to the extent that these could not be met from taxes and public loans, and the task of limiting other forms of expenditure and restraining the inflationary tendencies inherent in this form of finance was undertaken primarily by the government through direct controls.

Thus we entered the post-war period with a very restricted conception of the role of monetary policy and relying heavily on the direct controls characteristic of the war economy.

Progressively, however, the wartime direct controls were abandoned and, of necessity, monetary policy re-emerged as a significant factor in the economy. In the study of this re-emergence I propose to examine the changing forms of monetary action by which levels of expenditure have been influenced. For this purpose we need to consider:

(1) action which affects the volume of money;

(2) action which affects the willingness of banks to lend;

(3) action which directly affects expenditure by governments, businesses or individuals.

The volume of money in Australia fluctuates widely but, in post-war years, was growing rapidly. Factors which affect its volume include:

(1) the balance of international transactions;

(2) government cash deficits or surpluses;

(3) purchases or sales of negotiable assets by the central bank;

(4) changes in bank loans and investments.

In the years immediately following the war, our export receipts were very high and there was a heavy inflow of capital. On the other hand, we were unable to spend freely on imports. Bank deposits of those receiving payments from abroad tended to rise more than the fall of the deposits of those making payments abroad and deposits in the aggregate expanded greatly. This tendency for the balance of international transactions to increase the volume of money was a dominant factor in the background to monetary policy in the post-war years up to 1951/52.

The significance of monetary policy can be assessed only in relation to the tasks which face it and it is worthwhile, therefore, to summarise the general character of the post-war period from an economic point of view. Three stages are fairly readily discernible:

1945/46 to 1950/51. This was a period of good export proceeds and heavy capital inflow leading to rising international reserves; internally marked by rapidly rising public and private investment expenditure; generally an increasingly inflationary situation with growing shortages, rising costs and prices and, in the final stages, an unwillingness to hold fixed money assets.

1951/52. This was a year in which imports were very high and export proceeds and international reserves fell sharply. Monetary stringency emerged internally and there was a sharp check to public and, to a less extent, private investment. There was some unemployment and a general tone of uncertainty developed.

1952/54. This was a period of steady recovery, followed by a slow but persistent growth in the pressure of demand on labour and materials, although prices have remained relatively steady.

In simplified terms, therefore, the tasks of monetary policy were:

1945/46 to 1950/51. To restrain the growing pressure on resources while providing for a rapidly expanding economy.

1951/52. To allow the natural check to the growing inflation to operate but to prevent it getting out of hand and setting up a cumulative downswing in activity and employment.

1952/54. To encourage the steady recovery and, progressively, to restrain growing inflationary tendencies.

ACTION WHICH AFFECTS THE VOLUME OF MONEY

In Australia, fluctuations in the balance of payments are a major cause of change in the volume of money, but these fluctuations are largely beyond the direct control of the monetary authorities. Monetary policy must therefore be based largely on government financial operations and central bank action.

Government finance. If governments spend more than they take from the public in taxation and in loan raisings, there will tend to be a net increase in bank deposits since those receiving money from the government will have their deposits increased by more than the reduction in the deposits of those making payments to the government. In the case of the Commonwealth Government, which is the dominant factor in this respect, the net effect is broadly shown by the change in the volume of Treasury bills outstanding from year to year.

The figures show that, up to 1949/50, the Commonwealth Government was able to reduce each year the volume of Treasury bills on issue to the banking system. This reduction was made primarily from the accumulation of funds in the various social service and other trust funds. It is noticeable, however, that, in the years in which inflationary pressure was reaching dangerous heights, government finances exercised little, if any, restraint on the mounting volume of money. In 1949/50, the reduction was only £15m., and in 1950/51, despite a Commonwealth Government surplus of almost £100m., the deficiency of loan raisings to meet state loan requirements prevented any reduction in the Treasury bill issue.

This inability to reduce Treasury bills at so critical a time was due in part to mounting pressure for tax reductions but, more particularly, to the increasing demands of public investment programs. At that time the level of public and private investment was too high in relation to available resources, and consequently there was a heavy strain on the capital market, already weakened by the general inflation. Through 1949/50 and 1950/51 rapidly rising prices produced a reaction against fixed money claims. Investors became anxious to hedge against further depreciation in the value of money by switching to equities, and subscriptions to public loans fell away despite the continued liquidity of the banking system and the public.

The history of this period emphasises the importance of government finance in economic and monetary policy. It is clear that lack of discipline in public investment planning can undermine the firmest of budgetary policies. On the other hand, if public investment can be maintained at relatively stable levels, the variation from year to year in the cash surplus or deficit of the government can be a major factor influencing the money supply. In an inflationary situation this variation could easily prove the most effective instrument of restraint.

Since 1951/52, the public investment program has been relatively stable. In that year and in 1952/53, the government cash deficit was substantial—Treasury bills on issue increasing by £45m. and £72m. respectively—adding to the money supply in a period when it had been substantially reduced by the balance of international payments and when it was necessary in the first year to resist a tendency for internal activity and employment to be contracted and in the latter year to stimulate the steady recovery which was taking place. In 1953/54 the Treasury bill issue fell by £35m., exercising some restraining influence as the economy moved towards full employment.

The period since 1951/52 demonstrates the valuable influence budgetary policy can have on the money supply and, therefore, on levels of expenditure once reasonable discipline has been established in the public investment programs. No other element in monetary policy can exercise so direct an influence or involve amounts so likely to be significant.

Open market operations. In economies with developed and active markets for government securities and for Treasury and other short-term bills, the conduct of open market operations is one of the major instruments by which a central bank influences the money supply. Thus, when a central bank purchases a security on the market, there is likely to be a direct and corresponding increase in the deposits of the public with the commercial banks and in those banks' holdings of cash assets. Correspondingly, when the central bank sells assets in the market, the volume of deposits and banks' cash tends to be reduced. The central bank can, therefore, alter the volume of money and so influence expenditure by the balance between its buying and selling in the market.

In Australia there are limitations on the degree to which these policies can be employed. While the total volume of government securities issued is relatively large, there is not a large market for them in a day-to-day trading sense and large-scale transactions are clearly beyond its normal capacity. Consequently, in order to ensure the marketability of government bonds and so to maintain their attractiveness as a medium for the investment of savings and the funds of financial institutions, the Commonwealth Bank is frequently a ready buyer on the market of small parcels of bonds and frequently facilitates other transactions where large buying or selling orders are involved.

The fact that the Commonwealth Bank, together with the Commonwealth Sinking Fund, constitutes so large a part of the market, gives it special responsibilities and tends to limit the effective use of purchases and sales of government bonds for monetary reasons.

The short-term market, which is so important a factor in the City of London and which is of great value to the Bank of England in smoothing out seasonal and temporary fluctuations in the money supply, is non-existent here. In Australia Treasury bills are held only by banks and there is little short-term paper of other kinds suitable for central bank operations.

Nevertheless, some use can be made of market operations. The Commonwealth Bank has an arrangement with the trading banks that they will consult it before undertaking large security transactions. Similarly, the Commonwealth Bank can influence the security transactions of the Commonwealth Savings Bank, the Commonwealth Trading Bank and of its own specialised departments. Furthermore, some variation in the pattern of its market sales and purchases is practicable. Unfortunately, market operations by the Commonwealth Bank and Commonwealth Savings Bank were not an effective offsetting influence at the time when inflation was becoming most acute, that is in 1951. The reasons for this ineffectiveness are interesting since they throw light on Australian attitudes towards interest rates which themselves form a significant aspect of monetary policy.

There is in Australia a widespread conviction that interest rates should be low. This view is surprisingly held by many lenders as well as by borrowers. The reasons are understandable and not without validity for our economy. Australians are expansion-minded and look to the rapid development of their country. They realise that expansion will be expedited if enterprise is not burdened with heavy capital charges. The relevance of this judgment is increased because in our major successful industries capital represents a high proportion of total costs.

This general prejudice in favour of low interest rates was intensified by the events of the 1930s. Many were convinced that the high rates of the late 1920s were a factor in precipitating the depression and that the low rates of the later 1930s were a significant element in stimulating recovery. Then followed the war with a widespread conviction that low interest rates were essential to keep down the ultimate burden on public finance of the wartime debts.

Thus, by the end of the war, belief in low interest rates had almost become a dogma. This, together with the knowledge that the many who had for the first time during the war become bond holders would be unlikely to understand the normal market fluctuations in the prices and yields of government securities, made interest rate stability at the low wartime rates an important objective of post-war policy.

In 1950/51, however, the inflation had become acute and mounting price levels had come to be regarded as inevitable. Those holding fixed money assets, including government securities, became conscious that these assets were declining rapidly in real value even though their money prices were stable. A growing tendency developed to quit fixed money claims in order to acquire properties and equities whose prices might be expected to rise with other values.

Thus the market for government securities came under heavy pressure from sellers and prices tended to fall and yields to rise. The Commonwealth Bank found its purchases rising day by day. For the Central Bank to be a heavy buyer of securities involved adding to the money supply—a procedure clearly inappropriate in an already inflationary situation. The issue had to be faced whether the Commonwealth Bank would continue to push out central bank credit to bolster the government security market and so add to the mounting inflation or whether a new and higher level of interest rates had to be accepted. After a brief period in which the Commonwealth Bank bought millions of pounds worth of government bonds in an attempt to hold the market, the inevitability of the change was accepted and yields were permitted to rise to about 4½ per cent by mid-1952, compared with the wartime 3⅛ per cent.

This experience is very significant. There can be no doubt that our capacity to restrain mounting inflation was weakened by the desire to maintain interest rates at the low wartime level. Furthermore, it made clear that there are advantages in some degree of uncertainty about prices and yields on government securities from day to day. The development of a rigid anticipation of unchanging yields is a powerful stimulus to inflation. The development of a stronger internal market for government securities, less directly dependent on Sinking Fund and central bank support, in which normal market variations of yields were accepted as natural, would greatly add to the capacity of the Central Bank to use open market operations in the restraint of inflationary pressure. It is important, however, that such restraint be exercised while the pressure is still manageable. Once confidence in the future value of money is seriously shaken, the swing away from fixed money claims can make government securities unsaleable and face the Central Bank with a dilemma in which it must choose between a serious deterioration in government credit and an intensification of the inflation itself.

ACTION AFFECTING THE CAPACITY AND WILLINGNESS OF BANKS TO LEND

In addition to the effect of the balance of payments, government finance, and of open market operations, the money supply can be influenced by the transactions of the trading banks themselves. Loans to their customers and purchases of securities increase the deposits of the public with the banking system. Bank loans (and investments) have, therefore, a double monetary effect. Directly, they provide funds to the borrower to enable him to spend more and, indirectly, they increase the total money supply thus making it easier for other spending projects to be financed. Consequently, the volume of bank lending is a matter of major importance in credit policy.

The 1945 banking legislation clearly recognises the importance of trading bank operations. Those responsible for this legislation recognised that the great increase in bank deposits and in bank cash which resulted from wartime finance had placed the banks in a position where, consistent with the maintenance of traditional standards of liquidity, they could provide for an enormous expansion of bank loans and that this potential, if realised, could be a source of dangerous inflation.

The legislation, therefore, left in the hands of the Central Bank two controls over the lending policies of the trading banks which had originally been established temporarily under wartime powers: the Special Account and the qualitative control of advance policy.

Under the provisions relating to Special Account, the Central Bank could call upon the trading banks to deposit with it the whole or any part of the increase in their assets after a date early in the war period. In effect, these provisions gave to the Central Bank the power to impose variable standards of liquidity limited only by the extent to which total assets had increased. They have a good deal in common with the 'variable minimum deposit' powers exercised by central banks in other countries, but the greater flexibility of Special Accounts is a special advantage to a country such as Australia, which is subject to wide fluctuations in its balance of payments and therefore in the levels of bank deposits and liquid assets.

It was clearly hoped that the Special Account provisions would be an effective influence on bank lending policy and the Central Bank used its powers under them extensively. It is of interest, therefore, to trace the history of their use.

During the war itself there was little need for bank advances. A great deal of war production was financed by advance payments from the government and, as the war progressed, banks found their outstanding advances falling. During this period, practically the whole of the increase in bank assets was called to Special Account but over much of the period falling advances tended to be replaced by increased holdings of government securities.

If the expansion in bank deposits and assets had halted with the end of the war, the outcome, as civil production was resumed and arrears of development began to be overtaken, would probably have been:

(1) a growing volume of bank advances financed in the first instance by realisation of government securities but increasingly by releases

from Special Account;

(2) the gradual contraction of the amount in Special Account as it was absorbed into the normal liquid assets of the trading banks.

In fact, however, with the continued rapid increase in our overseas reserves, the deposits and assets of the trading banks continued to rise rapidly—clearly on a scale excessive in relation to the monetary needs of the economy even allowing for the need to restore normal sources of finance for civil production. It was necessary, therefore, for the Central Bank to continue calls to Special Account. During this period, some part of the increased assets of the banks was left in their hands but large amounts were called to Special Account: banks were, therefore, expected to finance their customers' increasing need for advances from the new funds not called to Special Account and the proceeds of sales of government securities.

During this period there was a very considerable growth in bank deposits and in bank advances. Furthermore, the economy began to show marked evidences of inflation. At the same time, pressure on the banks for new and increased advances showed little signs of abating and banks, having used up the greater part of their government securities, found it increasingly difficult to meet the requests of their customers within the limits set by the Central Bank's Special Account policy.

By 1947 a clear conflict of policies had emerged. Some of the banks were unwilling to keep their advances to levels which could be financed by the funds left them by the Central Bank, and the Central Bank, worried by the growing inflationary pressure, was unwilling significantly to relax its Special Account restraint. At the same time, it was reluctant to adopt a policy which would face a trading bank with the necessity of completely withdrawing from new lending—particularly because it was recognised that, in Australia, months elapse before a change in policy towards new lending shows itself in movements of actual debit balances. Some device was necessary which, while giving the trading banks time to bring their lending policies into line, would maintain pressure on them to do so.

The device adopted was that of Central Bank loans. Trading banks were not permitted to draw on their Special Accounts but they were allowed to borrow against them from the Central Bank but at a rate of interest (at first 3 per cent, then $3\frac{1}{2}$ per cent) which it was hoped would be sufficiently high to provide an effective incentive to prompt repayment. Whether or not the rate was too low compared with the standard overdraft rate ($4\frac{1}{2}$ per cent) to provide effective restraint, the fact remains that some banks were prepared to see these Central Bank loans grow to substantial amounts, reaching the peak of £68m. in January 1952, and the growth of bank advances continued unabated.

There is no doubt that this was a serious deficiency in the anti-inflationary policy of the time. Even when allowance has been made for the fact that the fundamental sources of inflationary pressure were elsewhere, in the swollen public and private investment programs, in grossly inflated rural prices and incomes and in the heavy speculative inflow of capital, subsequent events suggested that greater financial stringency could have been effective in checking these excesses.

The experience of this period draws attention to two important elements in the Australian financial system. Firstly, the effectiveness of any central banking power, however apparently great, depends upon the response which banks, members of the system, make to the exercise of the power. In some countries, the nature and extent of this response is predictable because of established conventions of appropriate relationships between liquid assets and total deposits which are accepted and used as a basis of policy by the member banks themselves. Such conventions have not existed in the past in Australia and, consequently, the Central Bank cannot anticipate, even within wide limits, how trading banks will respond to its actions.

Secondly, the period shows a difficulty, from the Central Bank's point of view, in the banks' control over their lending operations. The banks' direct control over movements in their advances is reduced to the extent that drawings may be made by customers against limits approved in an earlier period. A tightening of a bank's lending policy will, therefore, not be immediately effective. Even the rate of creation of new advance limits cannot always be changed immediately. This makes it difficult for the banks to adjust their advances promptly to the general needs of the economy, and in a period of rising activity can cause bank lending to add to any inflationary tendencies.

In the second period, 1951/52, Special Account policy had to meet an entirely different situation. In that year we faced a sharp drop in export income and a delayed delivery of swollen import orders. As a consequence, we lost, in one year, £400m. odd of the £800m. reserves we had built up in London over a decade. These factors had dramatic internal effects on the position of the banks. The deposits of their customers and their own cash fell sharply and they found themselves facing an acute shortage of cash.

There was a clear danger that this set-back could have deteriorated into a recession. While it was important that the effects of falling London funds should be permitted to halt the gross inflation which had developed, the danger of a cumulative down-turn in activity could not be ignored. In particular, the flood of import deliveries and the sudden check to retail sales had forced unwanted stocks of goods on to importers, wholesalers, and manufacturers. Some expansion of bank advances was necessary if widespread damage was to be avoided.

Consequently, substantial releases from Special Account were made to sustain the cash position of the trading banks and so enable them to meet the needs of their customers. Thus, Special Accounts fell from £578m. in May 1951, to £158m. in December 1952, and trading bank advances increased by £180m. over the financial year. A great part of the Special Account releases reflected action taken to sustain the trading banks' capacity and willingness to lend but a part was due to a change in the principles of Special Account administration of which more will be said later. It can, however, reasonably be claimed that, whatever doubts may have existed about the effectiveness of Special Account policy in the restraint of inflation, it proved an invaluable support and stimulus to the banking system and the economy generally when faced with the need to counter serious deflationary influences originating in the balance of payments.

It was about this time that certain basic changes were made in the principles on which Special Account was administered. By 1951, a stage had been reached where a very large part of each bank's more liquid assets (apart from till money) was held in Special Account. This situation had arisen because some trading banks were unwilling to base their lending policies on their asset structure excluding Special Account and consequently found their other liquid assets steadily depleted.

This situation was an unsound one. Trading banks complained that, with a large part of their liquid assets in Special Account, they were denied the opportunity to increase their earnings and so build up their reserves against their greatly increased liabilities, and also that the normal responsibilities of bankers for the management of their assets to meet variations, seasonal and longer term, in the demands upon them were being taken from them.

Furthermore, the experience of past administration of Special Account policy suggested:

(1) that the Special Account was a useful instrument in off-setting the effects on the banking structure of major factors affecting the volume of deposits and the cash assets of banks, i.e., major changes in the balance of payments and in the sources of governmental finance;

(2) that it was less useful in dealing with the more irregular and unevenly distributed factors affecting bank liquidity;

(3) that the effectiveness of Special Account policy, particularly in the restraint of inflationary tendencies, was greatly weakened by the absence of conventional standards in the attitude of Australian banks towards their asset structure;

(4) that trading bank borrowing from the Central Bank for other than short-term or emergency purposes was a serious source of weakness to any credit policy;

(5) that since the effectiveness of any Special Account policy depended upon the response of the trading banks it was important to increase their responsibility and their understanding of the purposes the Central Bank was seeking to achieve.

As a result of these considerations and after consultation with the trading banks substantial releases from Special Account were made to enable trading banks to pay off Central Bank loans and/or to purchase from the Central Bank other assets including Treasury bills and government securities.

This was the first step towards a general change in Special Account administration which had earlier been discussed in principle with the banks and which was subsequently introduced. The banks were informed that, in the future, Special Accounts would be used to offset as far as practicable the effect on the banking system of major cyclical changes arising from the balance of payments and from government finance. This would leave entirely to them the task of providing for seasonal variations in the needs of their customers and, subject to this need, the management of their more liquid assets would be in their own hands. It was emphasised that this system would work only if they accepted responsibility for basing their lending policy on their asset structure excluding Special Accounts and, to this end, they were asked to work towards, and to aim to maintain, a stable conventional ratio of liquid assets plus government securities to deposits of about 25 per cent, subject only to seasonal and other short-term variations.

These new principles are still being tested and it is too early to decide whether they will be successful. They are designed to give greater freedom and greater responsibilities to the management of the trading banks and their success will depend upon the degree to which bank lending policies reflect the acceptance of those responsibilities.

During the period after the difficulties of 1951/52, the banking system has not, up to the end of 1953/54, been subjected to great pressure. During 1952/53, with steady liquidation of excess stocks and with steady recovery in overseas funds and the level of internal activity, bank advances were reduced from a peak of £699m. in July 1952 to £593m. in April 1953. Thereafter, as stocks began to rise again and as the level of full employment was approached, bank advances began once more to rise. During 1953/54, the growth was over £100m. (about 17 per cent)—a rate of expansion which at a time when the economy was pushing against the upper limit of activity short of inflation gave some reason for concern.

Looking back over the history of the use of Special Account a student of credit policy can have little doubt that it is an instrument of great actual and potential value, especially in the Australian scene where more traditional instruments of credit policy are inevitably less effective than in more developed money markets. However, the success of Special Accounts has been impeded by two characteristics of the Australian banking system:

(1) The absence of stable conventional standards generally accepted by banks as to their own asset structure.

(2) The very wide seasonal fluctuations in banking figures arising from the markedly seasonal character of international payments and the flow of funds into the Treasury. These fluctuations tend to obscure more fundamental influences and therefore to delay the response of banks to changes in their own positions.

QUALITATIVE ADVANCE POLICY

The second power over the lending policy of the banking system entrusted to the Commonwealth Bank by the 1945 legislation was that of giving directions about policy in relation to various classes of loans. This power, like the Special Account, originated with the need to direct resources during the 1939/45 war to purposes essential to the conduct of the war.

A good deal of this discriminatory content—seeking to classify various forms of production as 'essential' or 'non-essential'—continued into the post-war period itself. The attitude is illustrated by the fact that housing and rural production were privileged forms of production throughout the post-war period. Gradually, as the transition to peace became more complete, this normative element in advance policy declined and it became more exclusively designed to restrain the developing inflation and its content was, therefore, more general and less directed at specific forms of production. In its later stages, its emphasis was to concentrate bank lending on the provision of working capital for current production, seeking to force outside the banking system the provision of funds for financing development, i.e. capital expansion.

This policy was designed to restrain the growth of private investment, which was a major factor in building up the boom conditions of these years. It was argued that if capital projects sought credit funds from the market they would absorb some of the pressure being exerted by the swollen money supply and the discipline of having to go to the market would itself exercise a restraint on the more exuberant. Furthermore, it was recognised that if these projects were financed partly or wholly from bank advances, they would add further to the volume of deposits and so add to the inflationary pressure.

The reasoning behind this policy was, I believe, fundamentally sound and something of the kind may well have been inevitable in any period of gross inflation. Nevertheless, our experience of the operation of the policy was not happy. It was a source of irritation between the Central

Bank and the trading banks, between the trading banks and their clients, and between the Central Bank and the public generally. It conflicted with many of the traditional practices of trading banks and involved them in unwelcome security problems. Their clients resented the application of general rules to their own particular cases which they were invariably convinced had 'special' features unknown to the Central Bank, and when the opportunity came in 1951/52 the control was cheerfully abandoned. Although the policy was a necessary part of an adequate anti-inflationary policy in the conditions of the time, our experience with it suggests that so far as possible a central bank should seek only to determine the general setting within which banks can operate leaving judgments of individual cases to them.

ACTION DIRECTLY AFFECTING EXPENDITURE

So far in this review of monetary and credit policy the types of action examined have exercised an indirect effect on expenditure. They have been actions which, by affecting the volume of money and the liquidity and attitudes of the trading banks, could influence the readiness with which potential spenders could obtain funds to finance their expenditure. The Commonwealth Bank can, however, affect certain classes of expenditure more directly.

Firstly, the Commonwealth Bank is the banker to the Commonwealth Government and is one of the sources to which the government looks for information and advice on monetary and financial matters. It can, for instance, exercise some influence on the plans of the Commonwealth Government in relation to plans for public investment and public borrowing. In the first of the periods under review, governments were reluctant to exercise restraint in their public investment plans. The needs were clearly great and in a liquid and security hungry market government loans could be raised without difficulty. This period demonstrates how the normal discipline of having to raise funds to finance development can be undermined by an inflated money supply.

This situation was cut short when, as a result of continued rising prices, there was a swing away from fixed money claims and the public became unwilling to subscribe to government loans. The first task was to bring public investment programs to levels which could reasonably be compassed within the resources made available by normal savings but, once this had been accomplished, it became important to ensure that the funds required to support these programs were available. It is interesting to note that in 1951/52 and 1952/53 the holdings of the banking system of government securities (including Treasury bills) rose by about £120m. and £125m. respectively—in the first year largely in the Commonwealth Bank but in the latter in the trading banks also. Thus the banking system played an important part in sustaining public investment and the demand for government securities in a period when they might otherwise have been exposed to acute uncertainty.

The Commonwealth Bank is in a position to influence the policies of the Commonwealth Savings Bank and the Commonwealth Trading Bank as well as its own specialised departments. These two banks— the Commonwealth Savings Bank in particular—are major sources of funds for two groups of activities which exercise a significant effect on general levels of activity and employment: semi-government and local government works expenditure and housing. While, over a period of years, the funds available for these purposes are determined by the flow of new deposits and the claims of alternative investments, there is room for modest variation from year to year in the light of the availability of funds elsewhere and the state of activity in the constructional industries. Thus, in 1952/53, the finance for housing from the Commonwealth Savings Bank, with some assistance from the Commonwealth Trading Bank, was the greatest on record. Similarly, in these years maximum support, both directly and by underwriting, was given to semi- and local government loans. In these ways the constructional industries were sustained at a time when other sources of funds had largely dried up and so stability of the economy was promoted.

Since December 1953, as the economy moved again towards full employment and funds became more readily available, it has been possible to reduce the funds allocated to these purposes without any slackening in the total activity in these industries.

It is important to realise that, by the direct influence which the Commonwealth Bank exercises over the family of banks of which it is the head, it is able, within limits imposed by their commercial (and, in the case of the Commonwealth Trading Bank, competitive) character, to influence their policy so that they contribute directly to the achievement of the objectives of central bank policy: the stability of the currency and the maintenance of full employment.

There can be little doubt that this direct link gives to the Commonwealth Bank a source of strength which can be of particular value in times when the economy is threatened with declining activity and employment.

CONSULTATION

Central Bank policy can be most effective when it is understood by and concurred in by the banks directly affected by it. This can be only if there is frequent and sympathetic consultation between the Central Bank and the member banks. Over recent years there has been a steady development of consultation both at the level of general managers and at the technical levels.

In this consultation the basis of Central Bank policy is placed fully before the trading banks and every opportunity given for the expression and examination of conflicting or critical opinion. Finally, of course, responsibility must be taken by the Central Bank, which is responsible to parliament and the government.

The task of handling the economic set-back of 1951/52 was made much easier by the consultation and by the substantial unity of outlook in relation to the problems facing the banking system.

CONCLUSION

The record of monetary policy during the post-war period is a mixed one.

The task of bringing under control the post-war inflation may well have proved beyond the wisest of monetary policies—yet there can be no doubt that Australian experience showed up weaknesses both in our understanding and in our techniques. Certain clear conclusions can be drawn:

(1) No monetary policy can be effective unless there is reasonable discipline in public investment programs.

(2) Such discipline is practically impossible to achieve in conditions of grossly excessive money supply.

(3) In the restraint of a growing money supply, budget policy and more effective open market policy by the Central Bank can be of great value.

(4) If it is necessary to counter a growing money supply, open market sales must not be subordinated to low interest rates however desirable these may be.

(5) Both Central Bank and trading bank policy would be given a surer foundation if there could be established a firm convention among banks as to an appropriate relationship between their liquid assets (other than Special Accounts) and total deposits.

On the other hand, we can be modestly encouraged by our experience in 1952/53 which showed that monetary policy can contribute to the maintenance of internal stability in the face of external shocks. I say modestly because, while the achievement of the period was real, we were greatly aided by factors in the situation (e.g. fundamentally good prices for exports, good seasons, and a strong undercurrent of internal development) which we cannot necessarily count on for the future.

Finally, we can say that monetary policy re-emerging as a significant force to grapple with these problems has proved itself useful. We have much to learn and many improvements in technique to develop. In these tasks we can be greatly aided by frank discussion and the widest possible understanding. It may well be that we will never wholly solve the problem of combining economic stability with full employment and development but it is a task worthy of our best intelligence and our utmost devotion. Those of us who are concerned with developing and giving effect to monetary policy, while realising that our efforts can contribute only a part to the total solution, can be assured that we have a significant contribution to make.

Conditions of
Monetary Policy
in Australia

SOME years ago I reviewed the development of monetary policy in Australia during the period from 1945 to 1953. It would, I believe, be useful to continue this review to cover the subsequent years up to 1957. This was a period of some economic unity and focuses attention on problems characteristic of the Australian economy. It was a period in which a short but sharp recession gave way quickly to economic recovery, a recovery marked by rising levels of activity until boom conditions had developed. During this period the task facing monetary policy was to determine at what point the rising levels of activity were becoming inflationary and to prevent inflationary conditions emerging or to bring them under control to the extent that they had in fact emerged.

The period is, I believe, particularly instructive to students of monetary policy because:

(1) the factors producing the recovery and the subsequent development of inflationary conditions were essentially internal in character (This was a 'home-made' boom rather than an imported one.);

(2) the danger of inflationary conditions developing was recognised reasonably early;

(3) while the inflation was reflected in the balance of payments by the steady attrition of our international reserves in 1954/55 and 1955/56, these changes in the balance of payments did not of themselves set up effective restraints on our internal economy. (Unlike that of 1951, which was halted by external factors, this inflation had to be halted by the effects of internal policy measures deliberately and consciously applied.)

THE RECESSION OF 1951/52

It is necessary at the outset to recall certain features of the recession of 1951/52 and the measures that were taken to counter it. The collapse of the Korean boom in this year, with the drastic fall in export

R. C. Mills Memorial Lecture, University of Sydney, 29 April 1958. Reproduced by permission of Sydney University Press.

prices and the sudden rush of imports into Australia, brought to an end the post-war inflation. The end of the inflation was precipitated by events which had their origin outside Austraila but which:

(1) reduced exporters' incomes sharply below the 1950/51 level;

(2) reduced the money supply and brought an unprecedented fall in the liquid assets of the banking system;

(3) flooded the consumers' markets with goods on a scale which produced the first post-war buyers' market and faced Australian manufacturers with a sharper taste of effective competition than they had experienced since 1939.

In the circumstances, these external influences could be relied upon to deflate the economy, which had been grossly expanded by the Korean boom, to bring some discipline into its developmental plans, and some competitiveness into producers' attitudes towards costs. The task of the monetary authorities was, therefore, to guard against this healthy adjustment growing cumulatively into a general recession of the traditional pre-war kind.

In this latter task the authorities were greatly helped by the inherent strength of the internal situation. Seasons continued to be good and export prices recovered to levels both profitable to producers and providing reasonable strength to international receipts. Furthermore, the strong undercurrent of internal private development persisted.

It is, therefore, not surprising that the action taken by the monetary authorities quickly ended the threat of depression and stimulated expenditure adequate to sustain full employment:

(1) The public investment program was stabilised at a reasonably high level and finance was ensured for it.

(2) Very substantial releases were made from Special Account, providing banks with the liquid funds to support a considerable increase in advances.

(3) Banks were freed from all advance policy restrictions on the character of bank lending and were encouraged to expand their advances.

(4) Through the various units in the Commonwealth Bank family additional funds were provided to sustain a high level of activity in the home building and general construction industries.

Recovery was rapid, so that probably by about June 1953 the economy was moving close to the full employment level. It is worth keeping in mind the various measures used to stimulate the economy since the effects of some of them persisted long enough to become factors in the subsequent tendency for expenditure to become excessive.

The recovery was first apparent in a rise of £147m. in personal consumption expenditure in 1952/53; expenditure on durable consumer goods financed by hire purchase was important. The effect of this increase in expenditure on production was delayed since supplies were drawn heavily from the great accumulation of stocks which had been built up in the previous year—the year of flooding imports. And in 1952/53 private investment still lagged, showing a decline of £82m., although it was soon to respond to the effects of increasing consumption expenditure.

Thereafter until 1955/56 there was a rapid growth of almost all classes of expenditure with the exception of public investment expenditure, which remained under reasonable control. Gross domestic expenditure increased by 13 per cent in 1953/54, by 13 per cent in 1954/55 and by 7 per cent in 1955/56; increases which greatly exceeded the increases in the quantity of goods physically available and which reflected also the rising prices which these inflationary conditions produced. In this expenditure the growth was especially evident in durable consumer goods and capital expenditure in industry and commerce.

Internally, the period showed the characteristics of inflation with which we had become familiar in the pre-1951 period. Shortages of labour emerged, leading to competition for labour and to rising wage rates, followed by rising costs, cost of living adjustments, and so on. Inefficiencies emerged again in the construction industries, where costs rose more than proportionately.

The internal effects quickly spilled over into the balance of payments. As expenditure ran beyond the value of effective production, it tended to increase demands for imports and to absorb exportable goods. It quickly became apparent that, despite reasonably satisfactory export prices, we had insufficient margin to provide for overseas expenditure at this rate. After an approximately balanced year in 1953/54 our international reserves began to fall sharply—not because of adverse seasons or low prices abroad but because of excessive internal expenditure. It was not until 1956/57 that restraint in domestic expenditure combined with a very favourable wool year to reverse this trend in our international reserves.

THE PROBLEM FACING MONETARY POLICY

It is reasonable to ask, 'Was it not possible for monetary policy to restrain the growth of expenditure when it tended to go beyond the level of full employment?' The question is particularly apt since as early as November 1953 the Central Bank had reached the conclusion that the economy was passing through the range of full employment into conditions where some restraint was called for. In present Australian conditions the net effect of the government's position is generally indicated by the level of Treasury bills outstanding, although in some years changes in government balances and investments can be significant.

In 1951/52 and 1952/53 the Treasury bills on issue had increased by £43m. and £72m. respectively, supporting expenditure directly and providing a significant addition to the money supply at a time when it was substantially reduced by the balance of international payments. With the change in the direction of the economic trend, it was appropriate for the net cash effect of government transactions to reduce the money supply in the three subsequent years. In fact, the Treasury bill issue fell by £35m. in 1953/54 and by £30m. in 1954/55 and rose by £5m. in 1955/56.

The government's budgetary policy, therefore, made a useful contribution to reducing the money supply and so countering the upward trend in expenditure except in 1955/56, when the net monetary effect of its policies was neutral. This may be a surprising conclusion when it is recalled that 1955/56 was the year of the 'little budget' when sharply increased taxes were introduced. It is clear that in the absence of these tax increases the government would not merely not have helped reduce the money supply but it would have sharply increased it, adding to the growing inflationary trends.

Of course, budget measures are wider in their implications than their mere effect on the money supply and the impact of these tax increases on imports and the rising levels of business investment were of considerable economic importance.

Some light is thrown on the problems facing monetary authorities when these conclusions are considered in the light of the bitter criticism to which these budgetary measures were subjected. It is a sad commentary on the level of political and economic understanding that action which was no more than adequate to maintain the integrity of public finance and to avoid intensifying an already vigorous inflationary trend required political courage of such a high order.

The apparently acute difficulty of taking specific budgetary action to restrain inflationary trends at the time action is called for does, I think, suggest that we should reconsider the rejection of some of the so-called 'built-in' stabilisers which were embodied in the immediate post-war financial structure. In the National Welfare Fund and in Export Stabilization Funds there were provisions which tended automatically to build up Trust Fund reserves in times of high incomes and employment and to run them down in times of falling incomes. With the long post-war boom it looked as if these funds would continue to accumulate indefinitely—but that fear is unlikely to be seriously held today.

OPEN MARKET OPERATIONS

When the Central Bank buys a government security from the public, the money supply and the liquidity of the banks are increased. On the other hand, a sale by the Central Bank reduces the money supply and bank liquidity. Accordingly, it is part of central banking technique to influence the volume of money and so affect the level of expenditure by its purchases or sales of securities. These are legitimate activities for the Central Bank and they help maintain the attractiveness of government bonds as a medium for the investment of funds of institutions and investors generally.

However, from time to time they involve the Central Bank in unpleasant dilemmas and can inhibit the prompt performance of its primary functions. While the Central Bank is so dominant a factor in the day-to-day conduct of the government security market, it acquires undue responsibility for movements of yields on these securities. Although it is helpful for the Central Bank to vary its transactions to smooth out random fluctuations in market yields, it is undesirable that its transactions should be determined solely or mainly by interest rate considerations.

In 1950/51 and again in 1951/52 the Central Bank found itself involved in market purchases on a considerable scale to prevent a decline in the price of government securities, and, as a result, pushed into the economy considerable amounts of Central Bank credit, which added to the inflationary pressure of an already swollen money supply. It would be pleasant to be able to record that when the problem recurred in 1954/55 the Bank was able promptly to resolve the issues and to avoid adding to the money supply—limiting its purchases on the market and accepting the higher level of yields which this implied.

In fact, however, while the character of the dilemma was recognised from an early stage, the claims of low interest rates and stability of prices of government securities were difficult to resist. The process of resolving the dilemma was slow—indeed resembling what in another context has been called 'an agonizing re-appraisal', and it was not until early in 1956 that Central Bank support for the market was reduced to normal amounts.

The net results of the Central Bank's security transactions were a fall of about £30m. in 1953/54 and increases of about the same size in each of the two following years. After the break in interest rates in March 1956, Central Bank holdings began to fall. Over the period this was a disappointing performance and indicated an inconsistency between the general policy being followed by the Central Bank and the effects of its activities in the market.

Delay in changing the direction of Central Bank market policy whenever such a change would involve the acceptance of lower prices for government securities is inevitable so long as the Central Bank continues to be so large a factor in the market as it is at present. In more developed economies, e.g. in the United Kingdom, the United

States of America, and Canada, there are markets which provide channels for large transactions, in which prices and yields are determined essentially by market considerations. Recently there has been a tendency, encouraged by the Central Bank, for such a market to develop here. The Australian economy has reached a stage where this can go further. It is desirable that there should be a number of firms participating in the market as dealers—themselves holders of government securities and financially strong enough to quote prices for a range of government securities. In such a market the Central Bank could operate in a way which ensured that its participation was marginal only and which would avoid it necessarily becoming involved for purposes conflicting with its basic policies. The adequate development of such a market may require the participation of more firms and probably a wider range of securities—particularly at the very short end of the maturity spectrum.

Effective open market operations by the Central Bank in the restraint of inflation are also unlikely unless we adopt more flexible attitudes towards interest rates. For my part, I accept what I understand to be the prevailing 'political' attitude of Australians of all parties towards interest rates—that is that they should be low. I qualify my reference to Australian attitudes by the adjective 'political' because in their private and business capacities Australians seem content, indeed anxious, to pay or receive interest at rates which to bankers appear abnormally high. Experience since the war suggests that in our pursuit of persistently high levels of employment and business activity we are likely from time to time to be faced with active or potential inflation which can be checked or controlled only by measures which involve the acceptance of a rise in interest rates—particularly on government bonds. Unwillingness to face this action would make periodical bursts of inflation almost inevitable and would increase the need to resort to more brutal methods of correction—such as sharp tax increases and the like.

When an investor buys, say, a ten-year government bond, he has a right to the interest promised, and his money back after ten years, and in the meantime reasonable certainty that he can sell his bond at a market price if he needs to. But it is unreasonable of him to expect also that he will be guaranteed the whole of his money back at any time, while being permitted to keep any premium that the market may offer him. The market now deals in a very wide range of maturities and the answer for those who do not wish to risk capital loss on possible realisation before maturity is to spread their purchases over maturities appropriate to their needs. If investors behaved with reasonable prudence in their purchases they would be less likely to be embarrassed by interest changes, and the government and

Central Bank would not be so hampered in their practices. Thus they would be the better able to protect the long-term value of people's savings in whatever form they are held.

While it is important that the public and political parties should regard interest rate variations as a normal and necessary feature of the market, those responsible for monetary action must guard against interest movements becoming a one-way traffic. In an economy where full employment is successfully maintained by a high rate of capital development there are unlikely to be frequent occasions when market conditions will of themselves produce a major fall in interest rates. Does this mean that we have to contemplate interest rates rising over a long-term trend in a series of steps—with the steps coinciding with measures necessary from time to time to check inflation? A glance at the graph of interest rates since 1945 would provide support for this expectation. We may need to be bolder in seizing opportunities to reduce interest rates if our development is not to be hindered by excessive capital charges.

CONTROL OVER BANK LIQUIDITY

Ever since the war, the Australian banking system as a whole has had a very much greater volume of liquid assets than it needed to support its lending policy—indeed if banks were able and willing to go on lending or investing until a normal pre-war relationship were established between the liquid assets of the banking system and its loans and other investments, there would be an enormous expansion in bank loans and in the total money supply, which would be grossly inflationary. Consequently, since 1940, the liquid assets of the banking system have been divided into two parts—the so-called Special Account, which is held with the Central Bank and is not available to the banks and therefore must be excluded from their available liquid assets; and those assets, usually referred to as their L.G.S. assets (i.e. liquid assets and government securities), which are in fact available and genuinely liquid. It is on these, their L.G.S. assets, that banks' lending policy should be based. Since the total liquid assets of the system are subject to violent fluctuations, reflecting primarily changes in the balance of international payments, it has become the practice to allow such fluctuations to have their impact largely on that part of the liquid assets held in Special Account, leaving it to the individual banks to meet normal seasonal fluctuations in their control of their L.G.S. assets. Banks, therefore, watch the movement of their L.G.S. assets in deciding whether they can afford to lend more freely. In making this judgment they must allow for the seasonal fluctuations. Banks tend to have very high liquidity in the period December-March when export income flows in strongly, when the Central Bank is financing advance payments to wheat-growers and when the government is a net spender. On the other hand, they tend to lose much of this liquidity in the April-June period, when tax money flows strongly to the government and export proceeds weaken. The task of the banks in interpreting their liquid position is made more complex by the magnitude and uncertainty of this seasonal movement. A more even flow in the receipts of government revenue and a greater participation of the public in the provision of the seasonal finance at present provided by the Central Bank would be of great value in evening out this movement.

It will be seen that the Central Bank can, by altering the distribution of the banking system's liquid assets between the Special Account and the banks' L.G.S. assets, affect the banks' capacity and willingness to lend. Generally, it is the object of the Central Bank's Special Account policy to ensure that the banks have sufficient L.G.S. assets to support an adequate but not excessive lending policy.

It will be recalled that in 1952 there had been very substantial releases from Special Account. In part these were due to the Central Bank's desire to support the banks in lending more freely to help counter declining expenditure. However, in part also they were due to a deliberate change in the policy governing the division between the two parts of the total liquid assets of the banking system—a shift from Central Bank-controlled Special Account to trading bank-controlled L.G.S. Since this change had profound effects later, it is important that the circumstances in which it was made should be understood.

By 1951 the position had been reached when a very large proportion of the liquid assets of the system (apart from till money) was held in Special Account. This position had been reached because some banks had been unwilling to base their lending policies on the L.G.S. assets alone and had continued to lend even when these were low and had to be sustained by borrowing from the Central Bank. The position was clearly unsatisfactory. Trading banks complained that, with a large part of their assets in Special Account, they were denied the opportunity to increase their earnings and strengthen their reserves and that they were being deprived of the normal responsibilities of bankers in the management of their assets. The Central Bank, on the other hand, felt that the value of the Special Account system was reduced by the absence of any clear basis for the relationship between bank loans and their L.G.S. assets, that it was desirable to confine Central Bank loans to short-term or emergency purposes and that it was important that trading banks should be permitted and expected to exercise greater responsibilities.

Following consultations with the trading banks during 1952, and on the understanding that, if a greater proportion of the liquid assets of the system were placed under their control, banks would ensure that they remained part of their L.G.S. assets and would not merely become a basis for expanded lending, Special Account action was planned so that the banks, after paying off Central Bank loans, could build their L.G.S. ratios to about 25 per cent by June 1953. It was emphasised that this new division of responsibility would be ineffective unless the banks based their lending policies on their L.G.S. assets only and they were asked by the Central Bank to work towards and seek to maintain a ratio of L.G.S. to deposits of 25 per cent, subject only to seasonal and other short-term variations. It was hoped thus to establish a convention of behaviour, similar to those operating in other countries, which would be a guide to both Central Bank and trading banks in their relationships.

Let us look now at the role played by bank advances over the period under review. It will be recalled that in 1951/52 there was an increase in bank advances of £185m.—a large part of which was associated with the financing of increased stocks of goods imported, although some part reflected the easier lending policies which the Central Bank had encouraged the trading banks to undertake. In 1952/53 there was, despite the easier policy, a fall in bank advances of £97m. The running down of the heavy stocks of imported goods, a somewhat lower level of activity in manufacturing industry, and a general tendency among businesses to tighten up their own internal financial positions were reflected in this decline. During this year the attitude of banks towards new approvals continued to be relatively easy. During 1953/54 advances rose further by £113m. The Central Bank had continued to encourage a relatively easy lending policy until about November 1953, by which time it was becoming apparent that the economy had recovered fully from the recession and was advancing rapidly again. At this time the direction of Central Bank policy in relation to bank advances changed to one of restraint. Despite this change in policy the advances of the banks continued to rise—increasing again in 1954/55 by £140m. Not until 1955/56 was any check apparent; in that year advances fell by £24m. and in 1956/57 by £26m.

There can be no doubt that the rise in advances of £250m. in the two years 1953/54 and 1954/55 was excessive and contributed significantly, both directly and through its impact on the general money supply, to the rapid emergence of inflationary conditions. However, the magnitude of this contribution can be and indeed has been exaggerated. The rise in 1953/54 reflected the working out of the easier lending policies of the previous year and showed itself particularly in loans to the rural sector and to housing. It was not the rise in advances themselves in 1953/54 to which criticism could be directed but the continuance of lending policies which ensured a further rise in the next year. Even in this year, however, some rise was justified. There was a considerable restoration of stocks which had been run down to unduly low levels, and expanding manufacturing activity justified some increased provision of working capital. However, it is clear that perhaps £80m. to £100m. of the increase in advances over these two years was excessive and also that it took place despite strong Central Bank pressure to restrain it.

Special Account action in 1952/53 placed the banks in a position where, if their advances had moved in accordance with policy, they would have been able to bring their L.G.S. ratios on the average to 25 per cent by June 1953. This ratio was substantially achieved. Banks whose ratios were lower than 25 per cent, if they were in fact observing the convention, should have pursued a more restrictive policy. Some of the less liquid banks, however, continued to expand advances and to dispose of government securities and Treasury bills. For some time the Central Bank was unwilling to discard its reliance on the convention. Its first response was to squeeze the trading banks' L.G.S. ratios further below 25 per cent, in the hope that the banks would respond. Its hesitation was understandable. Movements of liquidity are frequently obscured by temporary factors. Some banks were unaccustomed to basing their lending on their L.G.S. ratios. Some had expressed the view that 25 per cent was too high a ratio to be uniformly applied but nothing had been said to justify the Central Bank in concluding that the banks were not actively trying to adapt themselves to the convention, and it was desirable that they should be given time to adjust themselves to new responsibilities and to learn the techniques of management required of them. However, by June 1954, it was apparent that more forceful action could no longer be delayed if the rise in advances was to be halted. Consequently, the Central Bank was obliged to conclude that the urgency of the current problems did not permit it to delay forceful action until the problems of establishing a uniform liquidity convention were resolved. Accordingly, it proceeded to adminster Special Account so as to withdraw from the banks some part of the assets previously released to them. Even so, it was much less drastic than it might have been; 1954/55 was a year in which there was a substantial loss of international reserves, amounting to £142m. If the whole of this loss had been allowed to fall directly on the L.G.S. assets of the banks, their liquidity and their capacity to lend would have been abruptly curtailed. The Central Bank, however, felt this would be unjust to those banks who were effectively co-operating and was anxious to resolve this issue amicably. Accordingly, releases were made from Special Account totalling £71m., about half the liquidity lost through the fall in international reserves. This, however, was sufficient to bring the liquidity of the least liquid banks to very low levels. This action proved effective and it soon became apparent that banks had at last brought their lending under effective control.

The time was opportune, therefore, for a fresh approach to the question of a firm liquidity arrangement with the trading banks. The Central Bank could not administer Special Account on the basis of a convention until there was firm evidence of the banks' willingness and capacity to observe it. In the absence of a convention, it could only revert to the practice of keeping the least liquid banks with little more than till money and thus continuously dependent on the Central Bank for loans. This was an arrangement which banks could scarcely find palatable.

Further discussion with the trading banks followed and a clear understanding was reached:

(1) Each bank undertook to direct its policy to ensuring that its L.G.S. ratio would not fall below an agreed uniform minimum.

(2) Each bank undertook that, if for any reason its L.G.S. ratio fell below the agreed minimum, it would borrow from the Central Bank on terms which would be fixed by the Central Bank in the light of current policy and its assessment of the policy of the bank concerned, i.e. on terms which could be penal if the Central Bank thought this justified.

(3) The Central Bank informed the banks that it proposed to administer Special Account so that, if bank lending was in accord with Central Bank credit policy, banks generally would be able to maintain the L.G.S. ratios above the agreed minimum.

The working of the convention can be illustrated by the following example. If, following a period of relatively easy credit conditions, a more restrictive policy was called for, the Central Bank would, in addition to advising the trading banks of the need for a more restrained policy, administer Special Account so as to bring the L.G.S. ratios of the banks closer to the minimum. If the response of the banks was inadequate, more funds would be called to Special Account, forcing the L.G.S. ratio to lower levels—perhaps making it necessary for some banks to go into debt to the Central Bank.

On the other hand, if a more expansive credit policy was called for, the Central Bank would administer Special Account so as to increase the banks' L.G.S. ratio above the minimum and so provide them with the means and a stimulus to expansion. Movements in the L.G.S. ratio would thus serve both as an indicator of, and a support for, credit policy.

This new arrangement differs from the earlier attempt in two important respects:

(1) This plan is based on a minimum L.G.S. rather than an average. It relates, therefore, to the low point of the seasonal fluctuation in

liquidity and banks need to interpret their position at any other time with due regard for the run down in liquidity which they are likely to experience. It is more precise than the earlier arrangement and appears likely to provide a satisfactory working basis for Central Bank-trading bank relationships.

(2) It leaves in the hands of the banks a generally lower proportion of the total liquid assets of the banking system than did the earlier plan. This does not affect its value as an instrument of credit policy but it leaves the trading banks with an asset structure not wholly satisfactory. If a bank maintains sufficient 'quick' liquid assets—cash, deposits with the Central Bank, and Treasury bills—to provide for fluctuations, it will be weak in its second line of defence—government securities—and it will be sacrificing income. On the other hand, if it keeps up its average holdings of government securities, it will be relying perhaps unduly on the immediate marketability of government securities.

The first attempt to establish a firm liquidity convention was not successful. It would be purposeless to try to allocate responsibility for the failure, but it is worth while to consider what objective factors contributed to it. Looking back on the attempt I feel that the plan lacked precision in the obligations it placed on the trading banks and made insufficiently clear what they could expect from the Central Bank. It assumed that banks could and would be willing readily to adjust their practices to a system which required them to base their lending policy predominantly on their L.G.S. ratios. Furthermore, it underestimated the time lag in policy changes becoming effective and the difficulty of interpreting changes in the L.G.S. ratios because of the magnitude and variability of the seasonal fluctuations to which they are subject.

The new convention has been in operation now for two years and, although this cannot be regarded as an adequate test, experience so far gives modest hope of continued effectiveness. Banks have been faithful in their adherence to it and understanding of its working and the adjustments it calls for in Central Bank and trading bank management is steadily being built up. Its greatest weakness lies in the fact that it necessarily leaves to the individual banks the responsibility for judging the impact of our very variable seasonal movements on their own figures. A more even spread of government tax receipts over the year and a development of the short-term money market, in which the Central Bank could help smooth out major irregularities in the seasonal swings of liquidity, would give it greatly increased strength.

If the convention continues to function adequately, it will, I believe, prove to be one of the major steps in the development of our monetary system. It is gratifying that it has been established, after one false start, as a result of co-operation between the trading banks and the Central Bank.

QUALITATIVE ADVANCE POLICY

Experience of qualitative advance policy in the post-war inflationary period had not been the happiest. Those responsible for its administration were, therefore, glad when it could be allowed to pass into disuse.

This did not mean that banks were left without any knowledge of Central Bank views on the credit needs of different sectors of the economy. In the regular consultations between the trading banks and the Central Bank, the incidence of current lending was, when necessary, discussed and from time to time suggestions were made for shifts in emphasis.

The upsurge of inflationary pressure in 1955, however, required some return to rather more specific and more public forms of guidance. In July 1955, banks were asked not to grant additional advances for the expansion of hire purchase or instalment selling. In September, banks were asked not to approve new or increased accommodation for capital expenditure or imports and were asked to review large overdraft accounts with the object of achieving reductions in limits and indebtedness—especially where substantial long-term borrowing was involved. These directives were designed to strengthen the banks' efforts to bring their advances under control and to reduce the period of delay in making a change in lending policy effective.

It will be noted that the directives, unlike those earlier current, were in broad terms and left detailed interpretation to the individual banks.

Since May 1957, after inflationary conditions had been brought substantially under control, there have been progressive relaxations of the earlier directives with the exception of the prohibition of additional finance for hire purchase.

CHANGES IN THE USE OF THE MONEY SUPPLY

The prohibition of additional finance for hire purchase and its effects on the hire purchase finance houses draw attention to an interesting feature of the period. The purchase of durable goods—motor cars, refrigerators, radio sets, furniture and so on—financed by hire purchase transactions was an important factor in the growing levels of expenditure in the period under review. This is illustrated by the rate of growth of amounts outstanding under agreements entered into by hire purchase companies:

June 1953	£88·8m.
June 1954	£132·3m.
June 1955	£182·5m.
June 1956	£212·2m.

This growth of credit-financed purchases had a profoundly stimulating effect on the industries concerned and on the economy generally. Until 1953/54, hire purchase companies had relied heavily on bank overdrafts as a source of finance. Thus in 1953/54 nearly 30 per cent of their funds came from bank overdrafts. Thereafter, as a result of credit policy measures, there was a net decrease in their indebtedness to the banks. But the loss of these funds was more than compensated for by the great increase in funds obtained from sources other than share issues and bank advances. Some of these companies had already been relying significantly on funds raised by deposits, debenture issues, notes, etc. Issue of debentures and notes jumped from £6·5m. in 1953/54 to an average of £18·8m. in the three subsequent years. In other words, hire purchase companies changed the emphasis in their financing from borrowing from the banks to borrowing directly from those who had reserve stocks of money—usually in the form of bank deposits.

In the event, hire purchase companies generally found funds easy to raise and the need to go to the market did not impose any significant restraint on their activities. They were highly profitable enterprises and able to offer attractive rates of interest. They were, however, not alone in the field. Many business enterprises, particularly in the field of commerce, sought additional funds direct from those able to lend or invest. This is illustrated by the following figures for new money raised by listed companies:

	Share issues £m.	Debentures, notes, deposits £m.
1952/53	26·5	11·9*
1953/54	42·6	28·3*
1954/55	59·7	27·5
1955/56	59·2	50·2
1956/57	43·7	51·6

* Estimated.

This great flow of funds directly from those holding stocks of money was largely financed by a more frequent use of the existing money supply rather than from an increase in the volume of money itself.

As a first approximation, one would think it desirable that the money supply should bear a reasonably constant relationship to the value of total production. However, ever since 1946 there has been a persistent downward trend in the money supply expressed as a percentage of the gross national product and since 1955 this percentage has been appreciably below the pre-war level. Expressed in general terms this has meant that the banking system has been becoming a less significant element in the financing of the economy. This is not necessarily a bad thing—indeed, it is a natural development in a growing economy with its financial institutions evolving and becoming more diverse and specialised. But it does mean that to the extent that monetary policy relies primarily upon action through the banking system it is operating in a steadily contracting field.

The development is not without wider implications of some difficulty. People are entrusting more of their financial reserves to business firms and proportionately less to banks and savings banks than previously. In this they are encouraged by the greater reward in interest earned and the fact that in recent years they have not experienced any losses. Nevertheless the greater risks of this type of investment need to be recognised. Unlike banks, business firms are not required by law to conduct their business in a way which ensures their continuous ability to meet the withdrawals of those who have entrusted their money to them.

The development is having its effects also on the classes of purpose for which funds are readily available. Money lent direct has tended to flow to the borrowers offering the highest rates. The traditional borrowers—governments, semi-government and local authorities, housing societies, schools, churches, etc., who offer safety but lower returns and who have in the past been financed through the institutional lenders —have fared relatively badly. Already it has become necessary for about half the public investment program to be financed from taxation. Every day doubts are expressed as to the adequacy of the flow of funds for housing, for schools, and so on.

Is it desirable to check this development? Has it run its course? Can anything effective be done? These questions are difficult to answer. The growth of direct investment has been linked with generous rewards but we may well be concerned if socially necessary forms of capital expenditure have to compete with the rates offered by hire purchase companies and other similar borrowers, or if we have to finance them increasingly from taxation.

To some extent the rise in bank interest rates in 1956 and in 1957 was designed to increase the relative attractiveness of bank and savings bank deposits. The changes have had some effect but the basic trend has continued and remains a problem for the future.

GENERAL CONCLUSIONS

If we look back over the experience of these years, I think certain general conclusions about monetary policy emerge:

(1) The effective action taken to counter the set-back of 1951/53 involved expansive policies which took longer than anticipated to exercise their full effect and contributed significantly to the subsequent boom. This suggests, I believe, that we might borrow from the engineers the 'feed-back' principle—so that even while we are still seeking to accelerate the pace of the economy we are gradually

countering the acceleration, even before the optimum rate of activity has been reached.

(2) The task of restraining excess expenditure in the 1953/56 period was intensified by two institutional changes over which traditional forms of monetary action have little influence and which helped make available much of the finance for the growth of expenditure on durable consumer goods and on private, industrial and commercial expansion:

(i) a dramatic growth of hire purchase finance as a major factor in the demand for durable consumer goods;

(ii) the tendency for people generally to invest a greater part of their savings directly rather than to rely on fixed deposits, savings bank deposits, etc., as a repository for their reserves and the increased reliance by business enterprises on deposits, debentures, notes and similar sources of funds.

(3) Despite reasonably early diagnosis of the rising trends of expenditure, the government, the Central Bank and the trading banks delayed effective action to restrain the growth of the money supply and the flow of finance for expenditure fast becoming excessive.

(4) Budgetary policy, with its well-controlled growth of public investment and the prevention of a threatened cash deficit in 1955/56, was reasonably effective but a significant contribution to help counter increases in the money supply due to non-budgetary causes seems unlikely unless more effective 'built-in' stabilisers can be devised.

(5) The Central Bank will continue to be handicapped in its open market policies until institutional developments in the government security market reduce dependence on the Central Bank and until we become educated to accept changes in interest rates more readily.

(6) Effective restraint of bank lending was rendered acutely difficult because of the failure of the first attempt to evolve a liquidity convention; however, subsequent experience of a modified convention gives reason to hope that an effective instrument of credit control appropriate to Australian conditions is being evolved.

(7) The task of the banking system in regulating the flow of credit is made more difficult by the magnitude and uncertainty of the seasonal fluctuations in the liquidity of the Australian economy. Action to achieve a more regular flow of tax funds to the government and greater participation of the public in the provision of seasonal finance would be of great value.

(8) Despite hesitations and delays, the conscious application of policy measures finally restored balance to the economy; the objective must be to take action before cumulative tendencies have been established. It is probably wiser to act even before the evidence is conclusive—accepting the risk that it may quickly become necessary to change the direction of policy. Frequent small adjustments are

almost certainly better than allowing positions to develop in which major action is called for.

The record of monetary policy over these years is a mixed one—if it had been completely successful there would be little to say about it. But in failure, or partial or delayed success, there are lessons to be learned. If these lessons are learned there is, I believe, reason to hope that we can maintain reasonable stability in the activity of the economy in the face of causes of fluctuations essentially internal in origin.

Whether or not we can deal effectively with major fluctuations originating outside Australia and affecting us through our export income, or whether over a long period we can guard against the slow depreciation of the value of the currency which comes from a persistent upward trend in prices, are questions about which our recent experience gives us little help.

I have tried in this review to look honestly and objectively at our experience and to be frank in my discussion of it. I believe that the more widely these issues are discussed and understood, the more likely it is that prompt and effective action will be possible to deal with our problems.

Other People's Money

'**N**EITHER a borrower nor a lender be', said Polonius to his son when sending him forth to face the temptations of Paris and, no doubt, most of us would nod sagely and approvingly at this pearl of paternal wisdom. Yet in doing so we would be more than usually hypocritical, for it is almost certain that we are, all of us, both. Most of us have made loans to savings banks and to banks, to governments and governmental instrumentalities, to public companies engaged in finance, commerce, or industry. In other words, most people own bank balances and often government and semi-government bonds, and frequently notes, debentures, or shares of companies. Most of us, too, are borrowers—from banks, building societies, or life assurance companies to finance our houses, from hire purchase companies to finance our cars and other durable equipment, from our grocers and other retail stores for the goods we buy on monthly account, and so on. Those who are engaged in business on their own account would find a similar picture of borrowing and lending in relation to their business activities.

Over the centuries, community attitudes towards borrowing and lending have changed greatly. Once one borrowed only to meet misfortune and, in doing so, one became an object of compassion or of censure, according to the charity of mind of the observer, while a lender was widely suspect as an exploiter of human misfortune. However, as people began to borrow from one another to use the proceeds of the loan for their own profit rather than merely to mitigate misfortune, the image of the borrower changed to that of the commercial adventurer—active, creative, and bold—sometimes, it is true, reckless, but certainly no object of pity. Lenders still tend to be regarded with more suspicion —at best, cautious and parsimonious, at worst, grasping and hard-hearted. Since we are most of us both borrowers and lenders, what Jekyll and Hyde creatures we must now be!

As the use of other people's money becomes more respectable and more universal, institutions develop to handle the transfers involved.

Sir John Morris Memorial Lecture, Adult Education Board of Tasmania, 5 April 1962.

First, there are banks which offer primarily safe custody for surplus funds, sometimes with a modest rate of interest, but also serve borrowers as a source of borrowable funds. As the purposes and processes involved in these transfers become more complex, more specialised institutions emerge. These are of two kinds: firstly, financial intermediaries more specialised than banks, firms which gather other people's money, establishing their own liability to the people concerned and then lending the funds themselves. Such financial intermediaries include insurance companies, building societies, instalment credit companies, etc. Secondly, there are institutions designed to make it easier and safer for individuals to lend directly to the ultimate borrower or user of the funds—these would include stock and share brokers, the Stock Exchange, issuing and underwriting houses and so on.

This complex of institutions, which can broadly be referred to as the capital market, mobilises other people's money for the benefit of a great variety of users—governments and their agencies, industrial and commercial enterprises, home builders, and of course householders and others who need access to consumer credit. It is difficult to comprehend how important the movement of these funds through the economic system has become and how significant this flow can be in its economic effects. In the Reserve Bank we have conducted a study of this flow of funds in recent years, out of which a number of interesting conclusions emerge.

For persons and unincorporated businesses, savings were lodged 37 per cent in banks, 35 per cent with other financial intermediaries (life assurance and pension funds being particularly important), about 16 per cent in shares, debentures, and other securities issued by non-finance companies, and about 7 per cent in government securities. On the other hand, this group were substantial borrowers both from banks and other financial intermediaries (instalment credit firms, building societies, insurance companies, pastoral finance companies), with other financial intermediaries providing about 40 per cent of the loans, compared with 26 per cent from banks.

Companies not engaged in finance have, despite large savings from their own profits, been substantial net borrowers but have relied less on financial intermediaries than have individuals. Their financial assets (apart from credit extended in the course of business) have been mainly with banks and their borrowing has been mainly through shares and other capital issues, the major part taken up direct by individuals. They have, too, drawn heavily upon lenders in other countries.

Governments, like companies, have financed much of their capital expenditure from savings (that is, the excess of current receipts over expenditure on non-capital items). It is interesting to note that the Commonwealth Government has been a net lender and governments as a whole have financed 85 per cent of their capital expenditure from savings. Governments are substantial lenders—the Commonwealth Government to other governments and all governments to individuals, particularly for housing.

More generally, the following conclusions emerge:

(1) There has been, since the war, a very great increase in the flow of funds through the capital market.

(2) The greater part of this increase has occurred in the funds which have moved either through non-bank financial intermediaries or direct from lender to borrower through the making of deposits or the purchase of notes, debentures, shares and other securities.

(3) The proportion of these direct borrowings which have taken the form of loans rather than participating share capital has greatly increased.

(4) The flow of investment funds from abroad has become an increasingly important element in financing capital expenditure—particularly that of non-finance companies which obtained almost 20 per cent of total funds used for these purposes from outside Australia in the five years ending June 1958. Approximately two-thirds of this represented profits retained by Australian branches and subsidiaries of overseas enterprises.

(5) The consumers have resorted to borrowing through hire purchase and similar time-payment devices to an extent hitherto unknown. The recorded outstandings of retail hire purchase lending by finance businesses in 1947/48 was little more than £20m.; by 1959/60 this had risen to more than £420m. The annual increase rose from less than £10m. to almost £70m.

(6) While the pattern of post-war experience has been one of a substantially increasing flow of funds for lending through the capital market, there is recorded in 1960/61 quite a dramatic fall in this flow which is apparent particularly in one of the sectors which had previously grown most rapidly—hire purchase. Here for the first time there was an actual fall in the amounts outstanding at the end of the year. In the same year issues of debentures, notes, and deposits fell appreciably, particularly by financial intermediaries.

Although these developments in our money market are in a sense natural in that they follow the broad pattern of similar developments in more mature economies, they have been of such a magnitude and have occurred at such a speed as to represent almost a revolution in our financial structure. Certainly they have created and will continue to create problems for us. It is the purpose of this paper to glance quickly at some of these problems and the ways in which we are trying to deal with them.

In particular, I would like to consider the following issues:

(1) What significance has this development of the capital market to the individual in the employment of his surplus funds?

(2) What is the significance of the rapid emergence of financial intermediaries other than banks?

(3) What has been the effect on the economic system of the rapid development of consumer credit—through hire purchase finance companies and the like?

(4) How important economically is the flow of capital from abroad —and what should be our attitude towards it?

(5) What is the reason for the rapid growth of the total funds flowing through the capital market and of the fluctuations in this flow —such as the decline which occurred in 1960/61? Can anything be done to mitigate these fluctuations and their effects?

THE CAPITAL MARKET AND THE INDIVIDUAL

The increase in the flow of funds through the capital market via non-bank financial intermediaries and direct to ultimate users creates problems for lenders.

So long as people were content to entrust their reserve funds substantially to banks they had, in recent years at any rate, little anxiety about the security of these reserves. This is not because banks are inherently safe. Indeed, a bank is in essence a very risky enterprise since it takes money from its depositors in the main with a guarantee to return it on demand, while at the same time using the money so entrusted to it to buy income-earning assets and to make loans. Obviously, if a very large number of a bank's depositors sought to withdraw their money at the same time, it would be impossible for the bank, without assistance, to meet their demands.

The early history of banking is crowded with occasions when doubts as to the management or stability of some bank brought a run of its depositors demanding their money back. Frequently on these occasions the managements, even of banks whose affairs had been prudently managed, found it impossible to realise their assets sufficiently promptly and were forced to suspend payment. However, as a result of these experiences, most civilised countries now have legislation (or conventional arrangements of similar significance) designed to protect depositors and to ensure that banks will always be able to meet their commitments to their depositors.

Broadly, this legislation:

(1) requires that banks should hold a substantial proportion of their assets in highly liquid form;

(2) limits the freedom of action of banks in the choice of the assets they can buy or the loans they can make;

(3) establishes, in the form of a central bank, a source of emer-

gency support for banks, that is, a place to which a bank threatened by a run on its deposits can turn for direct financial help; help which can be provided either by central bank purchasing from the bank concerned assets which it could not sell readily otherwise, or alternatively simply by the central bank making a loan to the bank.

These rather elaborate provisions for the control and the support of banks have developed slowly and somewhat painfully over some 150 years but now, in all reasonably civilised countries at least, deposits with banks can be regarded as almost completely safe.

Other financial intermediaries or business enterprises to which individuals may entrust their funds so as to get a higher return are subjected to much less rigid supervision and receive no comparable assurance of support in an emergency.

This does not, of course, mean that other financial intermediaries are necessarily unsafe; but it does mean that lenders and investors need to be aware of, and capable of assessing, the risks which balance the higher return which borrowers may offer. Unlike banks, other financial intermediaries and non-finance companies do not promise to repay mainly 'on demand' but usually on specific repayment dates. Borrowers accepting such a liability to members of the public can be confident of their capacity to meet it only if they have corresponding assets which will be liquid at that time, that is which can be converted into cash. A borrower who proceeds on the assumption that it will always be possible to repay old loans by borrowing anew is heading for disaster.

And so, if you are thinking of lending either to a financial intermediary other than a bank or to a business enterprise which will use your funds in its business, you would be wise to look at the character of the assets which the intermediary or the enterprise holds. The test is whether its assets are such that, when the maturity date arrives, they will be able to repay, even if a lot of other lenders are seeking repayment at the same time and if it is difficult or impossible to borrow from other people. In other words, it is important that financial intermediaries and business enterprises who borrow should so arrange the timing of the maturity of their assets that they match the maturity of their liabilities.

One of the problems facing investors in Australia is that it is difficult, indeed in many cases impossible, from published balance sheets, prospectuses, or other information available to them, to find out sufficient about the timing of a company's liabilities and assets. It seems to me that accountants, stockbrokers, and, indeed, the authorities of the Stock Exchange itself, should use their influence to persuade or to require companies with substantial maturing liabilities to the public to publish regularly information which discloses the maturities both of those liabilities and of their relevant assets. It cannot be too strongly insisted that it is not sufficient for a borrower to be conducting a profitable business or to have a net worth substantially in excess of his borrowing liabilities. Unless liabilities and assets are appropriately matched in their timing, these will not guarantee that the borrower will be able to meet his liabilities on the due date.

This need for maintaining a proper balance in the timing of maturing liabilities and assets is not merely in the interest of the investor.

A business enterprise relying largely on borrowing needs to take care not to be misled at times when it is easy to raise money. If it is wise, it will plan its affairs with an eye to periods when people wish to be more, rather than less, liquid. This is especially important for non-bank financial institutions such as hire purchase and other finance houses, building societies, investment banks, discount houses and so on which rely largely on fixed term borrowing of amounts often many times their shareholders' funds. There has been an interesting tendency in the United Kingdom in recent years for such enterprises to form themselves into associations and to establish for their members voluntary standards designed partly to protect themselves against these risks of instability but also as evidence of their responsibility towards the people whose money they are using. These standards are concerned primarily with the maintenance of reasonable proportions of liquid assets and the appropriate timing of liabilities and assets. They also, of course, include standards designed to preclude unsound commercial practices.

There would be great difficulties in any attempt to supervise the activities of commercial borrowers, particularly financial intermediaries, in the same way as those of banks. The business undertaken by these intermediaries is infinitely diverse and the policing of the legislation would be complex and possibly ineffective. Furthermore, there is a good deal to be said for avoiding legislation which could prove unnecessarily restrictive if this can be done without harm to the economy and injustice to the investing public. The price of freedom here as elsewhere may be the voluntary acceptance of responsibility. Our experience during the last year has demonstrated the dangers both to businessses which rely upon other people's money and to the investors themselves when such responsibility is ignored.

NON-BANK FINANCIAL INSTITUTIONS

Why has the post-war period seen such a proliferation of new financial institutions? They are not, of course, all new. Pastoral finance houses, life assurance societies, building societies have long been a feature of the Australian financial scene. But hire purchase finance houses, investment trusts, land trusts, short-term money market dealers, real estate development firms, merchant and development banks, discount and factoring firms and so on are, if not entirely new, novel in their scale of operation and in the impact which they are having on the economic and financial scene.

It is sometimes argued that the emergence and growth of this multiplicity of financial agencies reflects the rigidity of official banking policy: that the strict limitations on the freedom of bank lending has caused the banks to confine their loans more and more to the narrow provision of working capital on overdraft and to contract out of more adventurous and particularly longer-term classes of business: that limitations on the freedom of banks to pay interest on fixed deposits have left depositors with too limited opportunities to earn a return on surplus funds and have encouraged them to turn elsewhere. Correspondingly, business enterprises faced by unresponsive bankers and concerned at the periodical intensification of restrictive credit policy have sought other channels of access to other people's money they need for their businesses.

There is indeed some truth in this view. Necessary though the periodical restraints on bank activities have been, there is no doubt that they have at least encouraged this tremendous expansion of other financial institutions and that every stage in that expansion limits the area to which official monetary policy directly applies. However, like most simple explanations, this ignores many important factors.

Each of these financial institutions is highly specialised—it undertakes the task of intermediary between the lender and the user of funds in a particular field or fields about which it possesses or aims to build up special knowledge or skill of a kind which a banker with more diverse responsibilities may not be able to match. The opportunity for such institutions emerges as the economy and financial system reach appropriate degrees of maturity. It seems, for instance, that the United States passed through a very similar period of specialisation some forty years earlier than Australia.

These financial institutions undertake also classes of business which banks, because of their special responsibilities to their depositors, would not wish to undertake and become skilled in the assessment of the risks involved. This is one reason why their charges are generally substantially higher than those of banks.

To my mind, therefore, there is a place for such institutions, especially in an expanding economy with a public increasingly able and interested to invest their accumulated savings. I do not, however, think that their presence makes necessary or justifies the complete withdrawal of banks from fields of finance in which these more specialised institutions operate; indeed the contrary. Banks, because of their comprehensiveness, because they get their money relatively cheaply, because they have well-trained staffs possessed of a wide range of lending skills, can compete successfully with these newly-emerged rivals, taking in many cases the cream of the business at more moderate cost. It seems to me desirable that they should aim to do so—both because this will provide an effective check on what sometimes seems to me to be the rapacity of the charges imposed but also because it will help keep a more vigorous competitive quality in our banking system.

For this reason I view with some concern the growing tendency for banks to participate as major shareholders in fringe banking institutions. Such participation may blunt the edge of their competitiveness and expose the public to exploitation.

CONSUMER CREDIT AND ECONOMIC FLUCTUATIONS

While I see a value in the activities of these specialised financial institutions, they can at times of rapid growth create acute problems for the economy as a whole. This is well illustrated by reference to our experience in the hire purchase field during the last decade.

It is well known that at some times people are much more willing to incur hire purchase commitments than they are at others. This wilingness varies, partly with the prevailing sense of optimism or pessimism in the community but more specifically in Australia with the employment situation. When labour is scarce and opportunities exist for supplementing normal earnings, either by overtime or by part-time work, people enter into hire purchase commitments with great alacrity. If at such times the capital market provides increasing funds for the financing of hire purchase transactions, very remarkable increases in expenditure on durable consumer goods can take place. For instance, during the years 1953/54 and 1954/55 the amount of hire purchase outstandings increased by approximately 50 per cent and 40 per cent respectively and, although the percentage rate of increase fell away sharply in 1955/56 and 1956/57, it remained at a high level right through until the end of 1960.

During years of rapidly expanding hire purchase commitments, industries producing durable consumer goods enjoy unusually high levels of demand. If such periods are prolonged for a number of years, as they were in the last decade, the firms engaged in the industry expand to levels only justified by abnormally high levels of demand.

The problems of over-expansion are intensified because of another feature of instalment buying. Just as people incur heavy instalment commitments when supplementary employment is readily available, they reverse their attitudes if these opportunities are suddenly and unexpectedly reduced and there is uncertainty as to continuing employment. The effect of this can be severe. Not merely are people no longer willing to enter into new commitments but they must continue to meet instalments from reduced family income. Retail sales will therefore be affected, not merely by falling demand originating from new commitments but also because part of the basic family income goes to meeting instalments and must be diverted from more normal expenditures.

There is no doubt that the sharp decline in the demand for durable consumer goods in the recent recession and the present slowness with which retail trade is responding to measures designed to stimulate employment and expenditure reflect the continuing effect of instalment commitments previously entered into.

FLOW OF OVERSEAS CAPITAL

I mentioned earlier that Australian non-finance enterprises had been, during the last decade, substantial users of funds from outside Australia. This flow of capital from non-Australian sources (partly, it is true, from the retention in Australia of profits earned by Australian subsidiaries of overseas enterprises) has become an important factor in our development—so important, indeed, that from time to time doubts are expressed at the wisdom of our growing dependence on it.

Over the last few years the inflow of capital has averaged more than £200m. a year and last year reached the record figure of about £325m. The importance of these totals becomes clear when it is remembered that over the same period our total income from exports has been of the order of £875m. a year.

There are no doubts that considerable benefits accrue to Australia with this inflow. With it comes often the benefit of overseas knowledge, managerial capacity, research, and marketing experience. Certainly manufacturing industries would have developed much more slowly had we not had access to these associate benefits. Above all, the inflow of £200m. of capital from abroad enables us to purchase £200m. worth of additional imports and so to divert our own resources to the production of other goods both for capital development and consumption. A study of the difficult progress of less-developed countries such as those of South-east Asia shows how shortage of foreign exchange for the purchase of imports is a restrictive bottleneck in the achievement of their developmental plans.

As against this, there are those who argue:

(1) we are building up foreign claims on our future income from exports which will become excessive and so embarrassing;

(2) we pay an excessively high price in dividends and interest for the benefits in know-how, and so on, which we obtain;

(3) we are selling control of our national resources to foreigners and so endangering our independence and security.

Weight is usually attached to these arguments according to prejudice rather than reason but it is, I think, reasonable to say that:

(1) the burden of servicing our foreign obligations is small relative to our international income;

(2) there are some instances where the dividends remitted are inordinately high—particularly in relation to the foreign capital actually put at risk here in the first case—but it is unfair to judge this question by individual cases; (When we consider the indirect benefits to Australian industry deriving from the more rapid establishment of an industrial environment, of a supply of skilled and experienced managerial and technical personnel, as well as access to results of research and development we could ill afford to undertake, the price overall is probably not excessive.);

(3) foreign ownership, despite uncomfortable concentration in some sections of industry, does not seriously impair our sense of national independence—even less, for example, than it does in Canada. (Yet there is probably good reason at this stage for looking ahead on this problem and overseas enterprises here may do well to make concessions to the prevailing sentiment in favour of Australian participation. For ourselves it might be wise to avoid setting up obligations abroad for the development of enterprises from which little national benefit can be expected.)

Probably a more serious problem arises from the fluctuations in the flow of capital and the degree to which this could exacerbate a balance of payments problem arising from other causes. However, this is a problem which, given adequate reserves (including access to the International Monetary Fund) and effective internal policies, we should ourselves be able to deal with.

CAUSES OF GROWTH AND INSTABILITY
IN THE CAPITAL MARKET

Generally speaking, the post-war period through to the end of the 1950s has been one of a substantially increasing flow of funds through the capital market, with an increasing diversification of the institutions which have mobilised and distributed these funds. The great growth in the volume of these funds reflects firstly a strong demand for funds from those in industry, commerce and agriculture who see profitable investment opportunities. On the other hand, it has been possible to meet this demand for funds:

(1) because the period began as one of excess money supply, with people on the look-out for profitable employment for funds they judged excess to their liquid requirements;

(2) because people's attitude towards what is an acceptable degree of liquidity in their asset structure continued to change, up to the

end of 1960 at least (with a minor check in 1952/53), so as to encourage them to favour less liquid but more remunerative assets.

Because of this latter factor, it is possible for the flow of funds through the capital market to bear very little relationship to savings being made from current income. If people are not merely increasing their assets with savings from their current income but are replacing, on a sufficient scale, cash, bank deposits and other liquid assets they already possess with debentures, shares and the like, this can make available to borrowers funds in excess of the physical resources available for the expansion and development of their enterprises.

In such circumstances, planned development will expand beyond what can physically be realised, wage and other costs will tend to be bidden up by competition, funds will be diverted into speculation in land and security markets. In other words, inflationary conditions can develop as indeed they did at various stages through the 1950s. For a while the rising prices and capital gains associated with such conditions encourage people to feel that they are losing opportunities by leaving any of their funds idle in liquid form.

Such conditions are of their nature unstable. An individual failure or threatened failure can cause people's expectations to be checked or reversed and the resultant scramble for liquidity can threaten even sound enterprises with financial obligations accruing.

Such a reversal occurred in the latter part of 1960 although we were saved from most of the really unpleasant consequences, partly by an unexpectedly strong inflow of capital, partly by measures taken early enough to check the worst speculative elements, and partly because, throughout, the banking system remained in a strong enough condition to sustain enterprises which might otherwise have been embarrassed.

It is part of the functions of the monetary authorities, including the Reserve Bank, to understand these fluctuations in people's attitude towards liquidity and to mitigate their effects. This is difficult, partly because of lack of information, partly because our formal authority is limited to the banking system proper, and partly because traditional monetary measures are uncertain in their effects on them. It does seem that changes in interest rates paid and charged by the banks in relation to those current in the capital market generally can slow up or expedite the rate at which liquid assets are turned over through the capital market. For interest rate policy to be a significant instrument of control, however, it would be necessary for rates to be moved more promptly and decisively than we have been able to move them in the past and, the desired result having been achieved, for the movement of rates to be reversed promptly. Political and social attitudes towards interest rates continue to make such flexibility difficult.

SUMMARY AND CONCLUSIONS

It has, then, been a characteristic of the Australian capital market in the post-war period that it has passed through a series of institutional changes following the introduction of types of enterprises and capital market practices that have previously developed in London and New York and other highly developed markets. These developments have caught on quickly here and have obtained surprisingly quick support from the investing public. When such institutional changes are taking place, such as that which occurred in connection with the growth of hire purchase finance houses in the first half of the 1950s, it is very difficult for any form of restraint imposed by the authorities to prevent the emergence of inflationary conditions. It is to be hoped that this phase of institutional development has largely run its course and that fluctuations in the future will be of more normal and manageable proportions. If so, it may be that the capital market in Australia will continue to serve usefully the purposes of industrial and commercial development and of rising standards of usage of valuable durable consumer equipment without creating quite such severe problems of instability in the industries concerned and the economy as a whole.

If this is to be achieved, however, it will be necessary:

(1) that investors themselves should assess more carefully the risks associated with the various avenues of investing their funds; should be more conscious of the dangers of increasing the proportion of their funds which is not readily available to them; and should realise that at those times when it appears most certain that capital gains will accrue to investors who forgo liquidity, the risks involved are probably greatest;

(2) that those who hold themselves out to accept funds of various maturities from the investing public should first undertake the responsibility properly to balance the timing of their assets and liabilities and to make available to the community information which demonstrate that they have in fact honoured this responsibility (It will be necessary also, I believe, for them to collaborate more closely with the government and Central Bank in seeking to avoid major instability in the capital market, even, or perhaps particularly, when they seem for the moment to be profiting most greatly from this instability.);

(3) for the community generally and those concerned in the capital market in particular to accept action through interest rates and by other means to restrain any tendency towards too rapid growth of the flow of funds through the capital market. (It cannot be too strongly emphasised that if the growth of the capital market outstrips the physical capacity of the economy and the market becomes distorted by speculative tendencies and unjustified exuberance, a subsequent reversal of the direction of the flow of funds to more, rather

than less, liquid forms of investment is inevitable. The deflationary consequences of such a reversal can be acute and long-sustained. If we insist upon enjoying a periodical binge, then we will certainly have a hangover.)

The Relationship of
the Central Bank
with the Government

N
O INSTITUTION which exercises significant power and authority affecting the lives of people can properly exercise that power without feeling itself accountable for the way in which it is exercised. This is true of central banks as well as other institutions but for them accountability is not an easy concept. To whom are they accountable? How often should they be called to account, and by what machinery? Most central banks these days have been established by legislation or in some cases older central banks have been national-ised. It can therefore be argued that central banks are responsible to the people generally through parliament.

But central banks work in a particular field and their actions bear directly upon banks and other financial institutions over whom we exercise authority most immediately although the consequences can affect the lives and welfare of people generally. But because our actions make an immediate impact upon the financial system, we should hold ourselves partly responsible to them at least to the extent that we seek to ensure that they understand the motives for what we do and are prepared to accept it without active resentment.

Furthermore, a central bank forms a link in a chain which spreads throughout the world and most central bankers feel that they belong to a family of central banks which accepts a moral tradition. We of the Central Bank should behave in conformity with the best features of that tradition and regard ourselves to some degree as accountable to our international colleagues for the quality of our work and our standards of integrity.

However, our prime accountability lies within the society in which we function, where the central bank exercising the powers entrusted to it by legislation exists alongside the executive government which has general authority for the conduct of national affairs within its own constitution.

It is now widely accepted that a government must accept broad responsibility for the economic welfare of its people. Since the actions

Fifth SEANZA Course, Karachi, 4 March 1964. Reproduced by permission of the State Bank of Pakistan.

of a central bank in the field of monetary policy are part of economic policy generally and have a significant bearing on economic welfare, it is obvious that governmental economic policies and the more limited activities of the central bank must be directed to the same purposes and be broadly harmonious.

A democratically elected government is directly accountable to the public. It has to give an account of its stewardship at the time of elections. Even governments which are not chosen by this process can be called to account if the public becomes strongly convinced that they are not behaving properly. Accordingly, governments are generally more immediately conscious of the need to justify their performance than a central bank can be, and a central bank itself must bear this in mind and recognise that the government cannot escape some responsibility for what the central bank does. In other words, the government and the central bank operate in the same field; the actions of each have a bearing on the performance of the other so that some degree of co-ordination of activities is absolutely necessary. This does not, however, mean that the government must become the dominant partner and deprive the central bank of all independence.

DEGREE OF INDEPENDENCE

The question of how much independence the central bank should have is impossible to answer precisely and uniformly for all countries. The traditions of one country are different from those of another; their financial and other institutions differ from one another. Consequently, the degree of independence of the central bank needs to be determined in the light of circumstances of the individual country. Every central bank should grow out of the local society. There is no prototype of a central bank set up in heaven. Rather they develop to meet the particular needs of their own country and their form and pattern must be related to those needs.

In the decades immediately after World War I a number of new central banks came into being. Often they were modelled rather mechanically on the Bank of England. Legislators acted as if every country had a highly sophisticated market like that of the City of London. As a result many of these central banks were not fully effective and exercised little or no influence on the pattern of events in their own economies. Indeed they had no roots in their own society. Gradually most of them have been modified by pressure of local events and the need to deal with local problems and it would be fair to say that more recently new central banks have been designed more consciously in relation to the economy of which they were to be part.

In general it can be said that there are clear advantages in the central bank having some degree of autonomy, if only because monetary affairs are highly technical. It is necessary to have people trained to understand them and capable of carrying through their mechanics. However, we should not magnify the importance of this expertise. In the old days monetary policy was a sort of mystery but those days are gone—or they ought to be. A central banker should be both technically competent and able to explain his actions to reasonably intelligent laymen. If he cannot explain, it may well indicate some confusion of thought and he may be well advised to think again.

Another advantage of a degree of independence is that the central bank can sometimes look at economic matters more objectively than can a government. A government with hopes and ambitions, prejudices and political theories tends to see economic events coloured by these intellectual and emotional predilections. A central bank can more easily stand outside political and social attitudes and judge more objectively what is happening. But a central bank cannot be more objective than its government unless it is prepared to free itself of its own prejudices.

This responsibility a central banker shares with other professional men such as lawyers and doctors who are trained, in dealing with an issue before them, to set aside their own attitudes about behaviour or persons involved. It is important that central bankers should think of themselves as professionals.

The third advantage which arises from a degree of independence is greater continuity. Governments change although the civil service provides a considerable degree of continuity. However, civil servants must accept broadly the general philosophy of the government which they are serving. A central bank is not quite so completely identified with the government. It can bring to bear on its problems knowledge built up over longer and more continuous experience.

Furthermore, the central bank is closer to the market place than the government and its administrators can be. The central bank is part of the financial system and is in daily touch with the men and institutions which form it. It can therefore be sensitive to the tone and feeling of the market to a greater extent than the government.

These advantages are considerable, but we must not pretend they are necessarily paramount. No problem is exclusively monetary. All have other aspects. Consequently, no solution to a problem is exclusively monetary and, therefore, we should not pretend that our expertise extends to the non-monetary aspects of the problems which face us and the government. A central banker should always be conscious of the limitations of his knowledge, experience and capacity.

A central banker should, therefore, be aware that independence, if too highly prized, can lead to isolation in which his influence can become limited and ineffective. He will do better to seek a partnership with government in which his role is significant but in which he accepts the limitations imposed by the need to maintain the partnership as an effective working arrangement.

The broad conclusion is that the advantages of significant working autonomy are sufficient to justify a degree of independence but at the same time a central bank would be unwise to lean too heavily on this independence. Indeed, the less frequently the central bank seeks to assert or remind the government of its independence, the more successfully the central bank will be able to function.

LEGISLATION

It is helpful to have the nature and extent of the central bank's autonomy embodied in legislation. Here parliament has to define the ways in which the central bank should exercise its powers and the relationship between it and the government.

To this end legislation should not merely set out the powers and functions of the central bank but should if possible give a broad indication of the purposes for which those powers should be used. In the legislation under which the Reserve Bank of Australia operates, it is stated that the Bank shall exercise its powers in ways which in its opinion will best contribute to the stability of the currency, the maintenance of full employment, and the economic prosperity and welfare of the people of Australia.

Without arguing for this particular set of objectives it can be fairly said that such a legislative directive can prove useful not only as a guide but as a protection to the central bank in the exercise of its powers. It lends the authority of parliament to the use by the bank of the powers entrusted to it.

Legislation in setting out the powers and functions of the bank should state clearly to what degree their use should be subject to the specific or implied concurrence of the government. In Australian legislation this is achieved in two ways. Firstly, there are certain powers, for example to fix bank interest rates which, it is made clear, the Reserve Bank can exercise only with the specific approval of the Treasurer. More generally the legislation defines the relationship between the Central Bank and the government in the following way. It requires the Bank to keep the government informed from time to time of its monetary and banking policy and provides that, if in the opinion of the government that policy is wrong, the Governor of the Bank and the Treasurer shall confer and seek to resolve their differences. If they fail to do so, then the government may issue a direction to the Bank to which the Bank must give effect. When such a direction is given, the government is required to inform parliament and to lay on the table of the House a statement by the Treasurer and the Governor of the Bank, setting out their respective views on the issues involved.

This pattern contains much that is desirable. It makes it clear that it is for the Bank to formulate its own policy but provides effective means for this to be reconciled with the policies of the government and for differences to be clearly resolved.

Finally, it imposes on both parties the discipline of a report to parliament. A report to parliament of a failure to reconcile differences would be embarrassing both for the Central Bank and for the government. Consequently, there is considerable sanction on both parties to avoid allowing a situation to develop to a stage where a direction must be given. In our experience, although from time to time there have been quite marked differences of opinion, no government has issued a direction to the Bank. Where difficulties have arisen the parties have proved to be anxious to work out a solution acceptable to both.

Above all, such provisions avoid periods in which there is a vacuum of decision in which no action can be taken. Such periods are particularly dangerous to monetary policy.

PRACTICES OF DAY-TO-DAY WORKING RELATIONSHIP BETWEEN CENTRAL BANK AND GOVERNMENT

The possibility of serious divergence of views between the government and the central bank is minimised by effective contact between them at all times. The ways in which this is best done will depend upon domestic considerations but it may be helpful if I tell you the way in which this contact is maintained in Australia. To the extent that the government and the Bank share a common view of the facts there is less likelihood of difference of opinion as to policy. The Bank seeks, therefore, to work together with the government in the study of statistics and the gathering of information and then in their use in assessing the total situation.

To this end I, as Governor of the Bank, endeavour to maintain personal contact with the Treasurer and with the permanent head of the Treasury and his senior officers and sometimes with heads of other government departments. We find that this can best be done with a fair degree of informality. I make it a practice to visit the Treasurer and senior Treasury Officers in Canberra and they call on me when they come to Sydney. In this way rarely a week would pass without contact with either the Treasurer or the Secretary to the Treasury. On these occasions the opportunity is taken to exchange information and to discuss current problems.

This informal discussion is supplemented by contact of senior Bank officers with officials of Treasury, both formally and informally. A number of continuing committees study such matters as the balance of payments, where the Bank and the officers of the government confer together regularly in order to reconcile estimates. This contact requires that the officers engaged are well trained, intelligent, and responsible and can be trusted to represent the Bank's views.

There are many aspects of the government's general policy in which the Central Bank has an interest but no direct responsibility. An obvious case is the pattern of the annual budget. Quite clearly the government's budget is its responsibility and parliament's; it is for parliament to decide whether it will be approved. But the budget can frequently involve the Central Bank. It may well provide for borrowing, which in some circumstances could involve borrowing from the Central Bank or the banking system. Consequently, in formulating the budget the government should be aware of the Central Bank's own assessment of the loan market and the general economic and financial situation.

More generally there will be times when the resources within the economy are not being fully used—when a stimulus is required to bring activity to levels of full employment. In such circumstances resort to deficit financing may be proper. At other times levels of expenditure are unduly high when there is pressure on resources leading to rising prices and in such times it will be highly desirable for money to be withdrawn from the economy. It is important that the government should be aware of the Central Bank's judgment about how far deficit or surplus financing would from a monetary point of view be appropriate in the prevailing circumstances.

In Australia we seek to achieve this in a concentrated period of analysis and discussion in the months preceding the formulation of the budget. Again this is done rather informally to avoid any suggestion that the Central Bank is sitting in judgment on the government's financial policy but we make sure that the government is fully aware of the Central Bank's views.

Accordingly, at the appropriate time we prepare an assessment of the total economic and financial situation, which is sent to the government and provides the basis for discussion. We make it clear, however, that the details of the budget are not for us to comment on unless, of course, our comments are sought on specific proposals.

Our practice emphasises the principles governing our day-to-day relationships with the government. The degree of independence given a central bank is partly a matter of law and tradition but the formal position is less important than the bank's effectiveness. It is possible for a central bank to be effective whatever the degree of formal independence written into its statute.

For it to be effective the central bank must command respect for its competence and its judgment. Its assessments must be justified by events and its loyalty to the government of the day must be undoubted.

Finally, its integrity must be above question. If a central bank is to command the respect of those whose activities it hopes to influence, it is fundamental that they should believe that the central bank is acting from honest motives.

The central bank is in constant contact with the commercial community and nothing will undermine its influence more quickly than any suggestion of dishonesty or corruption. A central bank, in whatever society, must seek to establish a reputation of absolute integrity.

Generally, however pleasant it may be to have formal independence, we will do better to rely as much as possible on persuasion and as little as possible on authority and to this end we should work to have more widely understood our purposes and the analysis on which our actions are based.

In Australia we have over the last fourteen or fifteen years devoted great thought and energy to educating the officers of the private banks not merely in the background to banking generally but in the theory and practice of central banking. We believe that to the extent that they understand these matters the more intelligent and valuable will be their criticism and the less they will actively resist the action taken. This is true also of the other institutions. It is important also to raise the level of understanding within the civil service, the government, and the general public.

I put great emphasis on the educational and persuasive function because I am convinced that no authority which exercises power can go on imposing policies which are thought to be unreasonable or capricious. Unless those affected can be convinced that what is being done is reasonable, sooner or later authority ceases to be effective.

Finally, a central bank must guard against the very real danger of intellectual arrogance. It is easy to come to believe that, because authority has been entrusted to you, you must be right. No man is infallible. Therefore, it is important that central bankers should approach their task not weakly or irresolutely but with a sense of humility and with the consciousness that they can be wrong. A central banker should at all times stand ready to listen to criticism and to re-examine assumptions and judgments on which his actions have been based.

Montagu Norman described in homely terms the proper relationship between a central bank and its government. He said that a central bank should be like a good wife. It should manage its household competently and quietly; it should stand ready to assist and advise; it can properly persuade and cajole and on occasions even nag; but in the end it should recognise that the government is the boss.

Financial Institutions
—Patterns of Change

D URING my term as Governor of the Central Bank, it was the
practice periodically to review publicly the developments in
monetary policy—to observe the challenges it had met and to
attempt to evaluate the lessons which could be learnt from its successes
and its failures. Those reviews, supplementing the annual reports of the
Bank, were embodied in occasional addresses by the Governor, the
Deputy Governor, and senior officers of the Bank. They make an interesting record—at least to me—and convey an impression of a struggle
to adapt patterns of thought to the changing demands of the time simultaneously with getting on with the day-to-day task of making the bricks
of decision while struggling to gather the straw of understanding.

However, I would like to look with more care at the institutional
developments—to seek a logical pattern and to speculate a little on
their effect on the theory and practice of central banking. I do this
partly because I believe that the task of reviewing the lessons of policy
is now one for my successor but also because I find the study of institutions of great interest—the elements in the total financial environment
which demand or make possible their emergence and the adaptations
which their existence imposes on other institutions. Furthermore, this
evolutionary process is not wholly independent of the Central Bank
and the government. As a by-product of their policy actions, they
can—and have—stimulated, inhibited, delayed, and moulded the form
of institutional changes over this period. It is possible, therefore, that
a look at these changes and the effect of official initiatives or inter-
ventions on them may give hints of guidance for the future.

GENERAL PATTERNS OF CHANGE

Up to and including the war period, the financial scene was dominated
by the banks. The range of other financial institutions was limited, the
market for government securities was narrow, and markets for other
financial claims were rudimentary.

Giblin Lecture, ANZAAS Congress, Adelaide, 20 August 1969.

It is, of course, natural that, with the growth and development of the productive aspects of an economy, there should be a parallel development of the financial mechanisms. As incomes and wealth grow those who own them develop a demand for a greater variety of assets including financial assets of varying degrees of security, term to maturity, and marketability. Thus a person comes to desire a 'portfolio' of assets ranging from cash in his pocket, money in the bank, through claims on various other financial intermediaries, semi-government instrumentalities, governments, private corporations, and on to equity shares, productive equipment, durable consumers' goods and so on.

On the other hand, the growing complexity and the different time horizons of productive processes, together with the possibility of acquiring consumers' goods on credit, ensure a range of borrowers ready to satisfy the demand for financial assets to be embodied in these portfolios.

Often, of course, lenders are also borrowers and the portfolio will include both assets and liabilities—indeed this would be the normal pattern.

This increasing diversity in the need for financial assets and liabilities is met in part by direct transactions between the parties but it offers also the opportunity for new and specialised financial intermediaries concentrating on bringing together borrowers and lenders of compatible time horizons. Equally it creates a need for markets in which assets constituting the individual portfolios can be liquidated and the pattern of the portfolio rebalanced at the owner's discretion. Such markets provide openings for organisational services in the financial field.

These processes of increasing specialisation of financial intermediaries and organisers have been characteristic of the Australian scene over the last two or three decades. Particularly during the 1950s, non-bank financial intermediaries increased their share of the total financial assets in the system very markedly. Between 1953 and 1960, the banks' share of total assets of intermediaries fell from 70 per cent of the total to 57 per cent. As a consequence it became clear that the traditional approach to central banking policy of concentrating its measures of control on the capacity of the banks to extend credit to the private sector —an approach bearing also the authority of its legislative charter— would condemn it to increasing ineffectiveness. If real influence were to be exercised on expenditure in the interests of financial stability, high and stable employment, and steady growth, the strategy of monetary policy would have had to be adapted to the wider focus of the financial system as a whole.

Progress in the development of the bond market and gradual relaxation of social and political rigidities towards interest rates enabled the authorities to develop more constructive influence on the flow of funds through the system. Thus variations in interest rates for government securities and for bank deposits began to be used to affect the amount and cost of funds becoming available to non-bank intermediaries operaing outside the ambit of official controls. Similarly, more attractively devised forms of government securities to match the needs of special lenders, and a wider range of deposit facilities offered by the banks, served to check the increase in the proportion of funds flowing to non-bank financial intermediaries while a greater diversity in their lending facilities kept banks more fully competitive.

This strategy, by keeping up the proportion of funds flowing direct to the government and to officially-influenced intermediaries, also reduced the risk of the Central Bank being forced into picking up directly or indirectly at some stage assets which dissatisfied portfolio holders were liquidating and also maintained conditions in which, temporarily at least, the quantity of credit being provided to the private sector from the banking system could be restrained. When such restraint was being imposed, banks would be obliged to hold increased Special Reserve Deposits or government securities, a course which was inconsistent with the sought-after freedom of banks to compete effectively in meeting the demand for credit. This dilemma has tended to clarify and emphasise the primary role of the Budget in sustained control of total expenditure.

Let us look now at the circumstances surrounding some specific institutional developments.

Finance companies. The monetary expansion of the war years, contained by continued rationing and shortages of supplies for some years after the end of the war, persisted, but, with the appearance of supplies, there was a demand for houses, vehicles, durable consumers' goods in great variety not previously available on the Australian market. Those with cash bank deposits and government securities were anxious to use them to acquire these goods, and those who did not were confidently prepared to go into debt—tendencies strengthened by the rapidly rising prices.

Concerned by the extreme pressure of demand, the authorities sought to delay the activation of monetary assets by quantitative and liquidity restraints on banks. Newly-emerging hire purchase firms found bank credit closed to them and the authorities hoped that the need to go to the market for their funds would discipline their exuberance. The first tentative approaches demonstrated that the incentives to hold traditional liquid assets such as bank deposits and government securities in such quantities were weak, and finance companies were freely able to bid away funds from the banks and the government and employ them in meeting demands which banks were, by policy direction, precluded from meeting. Furthermore, the official reluctance to see the prices of government securities, pressure-sold to many small holders during the war years, fall drastically, caused the authorities to support these prices by Bank purchases in the market—a procedure which clearly undermined the effectiveness of their own policies of restraint.

There is no doubt finance companies would in any case have emerged as a significant element in the Australian financial scene. They emerged the more quickly and the more explosively because banks were precluded from doing this business and because interest rate policy enabled them easily to outbid the traditional yields offered by banks and governments.

It is possible that banks would not, even had they been free to do so, have been willing and adept enough to make unnecessary the great growth of the finance companies. But the Industrial Finance Department of the Commonwealth Bank had successfully established a specialised business of this sort and was 'rearing to go'. It is probable that this example would have stimulated even reluctant banks into the field, some of whom had made studies of United States' practice in this kind of banking.

I still feel puzzled about this problem when I look back upon it. In a technical central banking sense, the 'mortal sin' was the refusal to allow the price of government securities to fall and interest rates to rise. If this had been done there would have been a real check on the liquidation of securities and fixed deposits would have looked more attractive. The severity of qualitative and liquidity restraints on banks would have been less. It is possible that we would have seen an orderly development of consumers' financing—in part in the banks and partly outside in newly-formed companies operating on a much less exuberant profit margin. But anyone who recalls the hysterical response in press and parliament to the first tentative moves to unpeg interest rates will remember that such a course was not practicable in the political and social context of the time. A long period of intellectual reappraisal and controversy was necessary, both within the official family and in the community generally, before such a course would become an acceptable alternative.

Before long, banks sought to restore their relative profit position by buying equity interests in finance companies or by setting up wholly owned subsidiaries in the field. More recently they have come to compete more directly and actively by making loans for purposes which had previously been the almost exclusive preserve of the finance companies. This may seem a rather roundabout way of achieving a result which, in the absence of official restraints, could well have been the natural course of events.

In their competition with finance companies, banks working with funds derived from their depositors are restrained by obligations which do not fall on finance companies. These obligations derive from the role of banks as operators of the widely used payment mechanism and serve to protect the community which uses it. The conduct of this mechanism is a source of strength and advantage as well as restraint to the banks and it would be hard to judge whether, even in this field of business, they are net losers by the balance of its benefits and burdens.

Apart from these factors there seems no good reason why banks should not absorb their finance company affiliates into their banking organisation. It may be that the present separation serves their material interests as 'two price systems' are often employed by monopolistic business anxious to expand their markets but not generally to reduce their prices.

Savings banks and building societies. Until the 1950s savings banking in Australia had been predominantly a government preserve with the funds derived from the depositors' balances being directed largely into government and semi-government securities and into low cost housing financed on preferential terms. The banks' decision to enter this field seems to have been partly protective—arising from the belief that the rapid progress of the Commonwealth Trading Bank derived in part at least from its association with the widely spreading contacts of the Commonwealth Savings Bank. At least the banks expressed great willingness to follow a similar investment pattern and it was not surprising that the government demanded this as a condition of its approval. This condition led to the establishment of the savings banks as legally separate from their parent trading banks although in practice this separation was little more than an accounting device to ensure the maintenance of the traditional investment pattern. Since then minor modifications of this pattern have been allowed, especially in permitting an increasing flow of funds into housing loans.

It can be questioned whether the separation of the savings bank business serves any useful purpose. It can scarcely be doubted that there is need for the banking system to provide personal savings account facilities distinct from a cheque account, and banks generally would provide them as part of their general services. Equally there is clear evidence of effective collaboration of the banks with the authorities in the investment of savings funds. The present separation perpetuates trivial statutory and other distinctions of little significance.

An additional reason for reconsidering this question is the effect of steadily-rising interest rates on the profit position of savings banks. If savings banks are to continue to compete effectively for small savings they must offer the currently higher rates on the full total of their deposits. The bulk of their assets, however, are at fixed interest or alterable only at longish intervals and sharp or continued rises can expose their profit margins to pressure. Such difficulties are more manageable within a larger institution whose asset structure is more varied and with a greater predominance of short-term securities and assets on which the interest charged can be promptly varied.

This vulnerability of savings banks has been emphasised by the competition of permanent building societies which, not burdened with the social policy of low interest rates for low cost housing, can and do compete aggressively for small savings. Since the difficulties they encountered in the 1930s, these societies have not, until recently, been significant repositories of savings, but have recently been making the competitive pace. They too, of course, suffer the profit squeeze in periods of rising rates, and the extreme difficulties of the United States Housing and Loan Societies in 1967 and 1968 illustrate that they can be a source of great anxiety to the authorities if their capacity to renew their members' deposits and to maintain a flow of new deposits is threatened.

Government finance. Not surprisingly the hand of the authorities is very apparent in the institutional pattern in so far as it bears upon the financing of governments. Developments in the last two decades broadly fall into two groups:

(1) Measures to maintain the attractiveness of the government as a borrower against the varied intermediaries bidding for the public's investable funds.

(2) Measures to hold 'captive' to the government funds from sources which have been traditional holders of government securities.

Into the first category falls, of course, the greater readiness to match rates current in the market for competitive types of issues but also the measures which have been taken to devise new types of securities to meet the needs of particular lenders. Thus the range of long-term conventional bonds has been lengthened to attract life assurance offices and pension funds; special bonds providing protection against loss on realisation as a result of interest rate changes have been introduced for small savers—a measure most valuable in freeing the hands of the authorities on interest rate policy; and Treasury notes bearing market rates have attracted to the government's seasonal finances funds available on short term to a wide variety of institutions and commercial and industrial firms.

These measures themselves have given significant impetus to other innovations in the financial environment. The ready availability of highly liquid short-term paper gave scope for the development outside the banking system of short-term borrowing and lending on a scale new to the Australian scene, and such transactions, once well established, spread beyond government paper to other types of obligations. By 1959 it was apparent that this development was well under way and that there was a danger that inexperience and lack of supervision could lead to unwise extension of this form of finance. The authorities decided, therefore, to recognise an official short-term money market and enable it to establish banker-customer relationships with the Central Bank as a means of exerting official influence over the subsequent pattern and rate of development of the market.

There can be little doubt that official action has both stimulated institutional developments which have led to the effective mobilisation of short-term financial resources and have ensured that a significant proportion of those resources is available to the government itself.

Some of the measures which hold 'captive' certain classes of investable funds arise from action taken for other purposes. Thus the convention negotiated by the Central Bank with the trading banks that they will hold a minimum ratio of liquid and government security assets was designed partly as a protection to depositors and partly to provide a firm base against which pressure on banks' lending capacity exerted by changes in the statutory reserve deposit ratios could be made more effective. It none the less preserves to the public sector a substantial, if irregular, flow of funds from the deposits of bank customers. Similar liquidity and control elements are involved to a lesser degree in the statutory requirement that savings banks shall hold 65 per cent of their assets in deposits with the Reserve Bank and government securities, the portfolio requirements imposed upon the short-term money market dealers and the taxation incentives which induce life offices and pension funds to hold 30 per cent of their assets in government and semi-government securities. Their primary effect, however, is to preempt the relevant funds for the government's borrowing needs.

These measures are sometimes criticised as undesirable substitutes for action which would make government securities the voluntary choice of the investors or as an undisclosed system of taxes and subsidies changing the profitability of the institutions concerned. These changes are generally marginal but we have noted that in the instance of savings banks they could conceivably prove a real embarrassment. These criticisms are probably sufficiently valid to suggest that such measures should be carefully scrutinised so as to ensure that the national purposes served justify the interference with the normal processes of the market.

Recent actions such as the elimination from all new issues of the 10 per cent tax rebate on interest earned on Commonwealth bonds, and the widening of the range of discretion left to money market dealers in the make-up of their portfolios, may reflect a greater willingness on the part of the authorities to operate within the market.

Inter-company borrowing and commercial bills. Another instance of innovation bearing more closely on the traditional interests of banks which occurred without official stimulus or restraint was the growth of inter-company borrowing during the late 1950s and early 1960s. A significant margin between banks' borrowing and lending rates of interest offered companies a chance to lend direct to each other on terms which gave the lender a better return than a fixed deposit and the borrower a rate lower than the overdraft rate. The risk of the loan being unexpectedly called for repayment was often covered by the borrower having an undrawn limit with his banker as a backstop —although skilful organisers of these loans were generally aware which of the major companies were likely to be in temporary surplus of funds and where to turn for replacement of funds recalled.

Banks reacted by instituting a charge for undrawn limits and later by developing greater flexibility in their deposit facilities, including the establishment of marketable certificates of deposit, and in their interest policies, but the system of inter-company borrowing seems likely to persist as a permanent encroachment on the traditional functions of the banks.

Moves to develop independent facilities to engage in commercial bill financing have not produced great response in the absence of official backing of the kind given to the short-term money market, and banks have been able to adapt their practices sufficiently to keep the bulk of bill finance within the structure of the banks themselves.

Longer-term financing. One of the areas of most rapid growth and financial innovation has been among the intermediaries concerned with long-term finance such as life offices, pension funds, building societies, and savings banks, whose total assets have grown consistently at rates around 10 per cent per annum and more, compared with an average growth rate of all financial institutions of about 8 per cent. Nevertheless, the early stages of the current investment boom in mining revealed inadequacies in the Australian capital market's capacity to finance and organise large projects. This fact has intensified the tendency for this sector of industry to rely on overseas capital. Whatever may be thought about the wisdom of non-Australian ownership, it is clearly undesirable that Australian investors should be denied equity and other capital participation in this field because of institutional weaknesses.

One move by local banking interests to help remedy these deficiencies has been the establishment of the Australian Resources Development Bank which, in significant respects, breaks new ground in banking operations. The Bank aims to meet the needs of large-scale enterprises for that section of their financial needs which falls within the 5-10 year maturity range. Backed by the eight major Australian trading banks, two state banks, and (during its establishment phase) by the Reserve Bank, it has offered its own obligations for a structure of liabilities ranging up to these terms and has found a ready response.

Parallel with this development there has been a crop of organisa- tional firms—the so-called merchant bankers—often with strong over- seas associations, whose function it is to mobilise capital funds from a variety of sources, domestic and international, to meet the needs of major projects.

If the current desire for greater Australian participation in the equity of mining and other large-scale enterprises is to be realised it may be necessary (since savings are limited) to divert funds from channels through which they normally flow such as housing, government and semi-government securities. If this is not to cause problems in these fields of expenditure, support for them might be sought from foreign sources. There may be room for further financial innovation in arrang- ing such a redistribution of domestic and overseas capital resources.

Foreign banks and foreign exchange. Two areas where the authorities have successfully resisted the pressure for financial innovation have been the establishment of branches of foreign banks in Australia and the control of foreign exchange transactions.

It has, since the war, continued to be the firm policy of successive governments not to permit the entry of additional overseas banks to conduct business here nor to allow overseas interests to acquire sub- stantial interests in any Australian bank. It has been urged that foreign banks would bring no significant increase in service or efficiency and would unfairly 'pick the eyes' out of the business, ignoring the national range of services, many unprofitable, expected from banks. More fun- damentally, the banking system has been seen almost as a social ser- vice—as a voluntary part of the instruments of public policy in the financial field—and it is doubted whether foreign banks would accept this responsibility. Accordingly it is feared that their entry could impair the effectiveness of the present collaboration between the banks and the authorities.

Against this it can be argued that it is contrary to public policy to give so absolute a protection to any industry—a protection likely to provide a cover for inefficiency. More fundamentally, it is possible to dispute the 'social service' view of banks' responsibilities and to argue that the public interest is best served by uninhibited competition and a minimum of regulation by statutory or voluntary means. Finally, it is argued that the ban is in substance ineffective since it merely means that foreign banks enter as part of the 'non-bank intermediary' sector and provide services in large part similar to those of banks.

A choice between these alternative views is essentially one of political and social philosophy rather than of economic or technical judgment.

Perhaps more surprising is the fact that overseas exchange business continues to be conducted solely by banks acting as agents for the Reserve Bank. This system, which gives them a virtual monopoly at fixed and profitable prices, with the risk of rate variation being borne by the Reserve Bank, is naturally enough favoured by the banks and apparently meets the needs of the commercial community. Compared with the fiercely competitive and ulcer-producing conduct of this business in the financial centres of Europe and America this must seem to visitors a blessed haven of privilege.

CONCLUSIONS

Could I attempt at this stage to draw together the elements in this rather cursory review of recent financial innovation and to suggest certain broad conclusions.

(1) The period since the end of the war has been for Australia one of rapid and varied innovation of financial institutions. The innovations were triggered off by the pressure of bank deposits and government security holdings built up during the war to levels beyond the portfolio wishes of many of the public, and have been maintained by the special financing needs of the growing durable consumers' goods industries and industrial and mining developments on a wide scale, as well as by the success of newly established financial intermediaries in meeting the needs of borrowers and lenders in special categories.

(2) The authorities, disturbed by the inflationary pressure created by expenditure financed by funds coming to non-bank financial intermediaries, sought to restrain credit provision by banks, thus inhibiting their capacity to compete with the newcomers. Subsequent use of interest rates, especially on government securities and bank deposits, as a check on the flow of funds to non-bank intermediaries, restored competitiveness to banks and it is now an object of policy to maintain banks as a large and significant element in the total financial scene.

(3) Indeed we seem to be moving towards a conception of banks as functionally diverse intermediaries inter-penetrating the financial system in almost all classes of business, providing a competitive and functional check on non-banks and, in return for their monopoly of the payments mechanism and their special banker-customer relationship with the Reserve Bank, adapting their policies, both in the pursuit of funds and in providing finance, to the demands of public policy.

(4) Such a conception, so far imperfectly realised, implies the further development of central banking techniques on lines which bear little relationship to the conception of central banking which inspired

the present legislation. They are increasingly techniques which recognise banks as part of a total financial system and place special emphasis on measures which affect the system as a whole and which cause shifts of funds between the officially influenced and non-official sections of the financial system.

(5) The development of these techniques requires a deeper understanding of the financial system as a whole. Theory, although it has provided a reasonable description of the workings of the system, has so far failed to provide a basis for prediction and the statistics of the flow of funds through the system remain a record of the past rather than an effective basis for forecasting. Such a deeper understanding should effectively underlie any general rewriting of the legislative basis for the Reserve Bank's operations—although there are minor anachronisms which unnecessarily inhibit the banks in competing in certain areas of financial intermediation which could be reviewed.

The Banking System
and New Guinea

T HE banking system in the Territories of Papua and New Guinea consists of four commercial banks, three of them conducting savings banks as well as normal commercial banking. Two of these banks were established before the war although during hostilities all branches were closed. Basically, this banking system has been developed to serve the needs of the white community in New Guinea, the Administration, businesses and individuals, although the Commonwealth Savings Bank has always sought to develop its function as a mobiliser of the money savings of the indigenous peoples. In recent years the other banks conducting savings bank business have also sought the deposits of natives in savings bank accounts.

Until recently, apart from loans to local businesses and to individuals within the Territories, which have represented a somewhat smaller proportion of locally gathered deposits than would be normal for the Australian business of these banks, funds gathered in New Guinea have tended to be merged with the normal investments and loans of the banks concerned.

THE SPATE-BELSHAW-SWAN REPORT

The Commonwealth Bank was stimulated to take a closer interest in the role of the banking system in New Guinea by the report prepared within the Australian National University by Professors Spate, Belshaw, and Swan in 1953, which was mildly critical of the limited contribution of the banking system in furthering New Guinea development, particularly among the indigenous peoples. This report argued that it was desirable and possible to develop the New Guinea economy primarily on the basis of native agriculture. Following the study of this report, the Commonwealth Bank conferred with the Department of Territories and the Administration and explored at first hand the possibilities of more active policies, particularly in relation to the

Address to the New Guinea Society, Canberra, 13 October 1960.

native peoples. The results of that exploration were substantially negative. The conclusion was reached, I believe justly, that there were few opportunities at that stage for promoting more rapid development of the native economy by the use of credit. Such possibilities of development as were immediately evident could, it was believed, be carried through by resources already available and provision of credit at that stage of the economic and financial development of the people was likely to do more harm than good. However, it was decided that the Bank should act indirectly to stimulate financial understanding and to encourage the growth of those institutions among the indigenous people which gave promise for future development.

Steps were taken for the savings bank to become more active in the mobilisation of savings and in increasing the understanding among the indigenes of the benefits of holding their monetary reserves in the form of savings bank deposits rather than in private hoards. On the institutional side, it was felt that the local government councils and the emerging co-operatives offered the best prospects of giving experience in financial and commercial matters to the local people. The Bank set itself, therefore, actively to develop its contacts with the local councils and their financial officers and to watch their development so as to be ready should any of them reach a stage where the use of credit could become appropriate. The co-operative movement was clearly struggling with difficulties arising from insufficient and inadequately trained staff. The Bank accordingly collaborated with the Administration by providing funds for the establishment of a training school for clerks, managers, inspectors, and so on, of co-operatives. Finally, it was decided that the time had come for a start to be made in the employment of indigenes in the work of the Bank itself.

On the whole, this program has been modestly successful. The number of savings bank accounts and the total of depositors' balances have grown steadily and effective contact has been made with a larger proportion of the village communities. With the entry of other banks into the savings bank field, this work has been stimulated by their competition. The financial and commercial activities of local government councils have grown steadily and their affairs have been conducted generally with efficiency. In a few cases they have been enabled, by the use of credit, to acquire motor vehicles which have been employed in their commercial activities. By far the most exciting development in this field has been the Tolai cacao project. Under this scheme a group of local government councils in the Gazelle Peninsula have collaborated to establish a number of fermenteries for the treatment of cacao beans grown in districts under their control. This industry is an important and rapidly growing one and native income in the Peninsula from this source is already approaching £250,000 annually and is growing rapidly. After negotiations in which several banks expressed willingness to provide the funds, the building of the fermenteries was financed by a loan to the native government councils by the Bank of New South Wales, the loan being guaranteed by the Administration. The project has been well managed and the councils have been able to service the debt in accordance with arrangements. This is certainly the biggest and most promising experiment yet undertaken in the use of credit for the indigenous people in the New Guinea economy. Similarly, the co-operative movement, despite a serious setback in the Gazelle Peninsula, following difficulties which arose from causes having no connection with the indigenous people themselves, has gone from strength to strength. The staff being trained in the school established for this purpose are proving efficient and it seems likely that the co-operatives will play an increasing role in the trading and productive sides of the New Guinea economy.

The native staff taken into the Commonwealth Savings Bank were chosen from among those being educated by the Administration primarily to meet the needs of the Education Department. Special measures were taken to teach the boys the mechanical processes involved in savings bank work and also to give them a better understanding of its organisation and functions. These staff members have now reached a stage in their development where they are capable of conducting the whole of the savings bank activities so far as these concern the indigenous people. It does seem, however, that, if a satisfactory future career is to be available to them, they must be given the opportunity to undertake more varied and more difficult aspects of banking work, including that associated with commercial banking.

THE THOMAS-RYAN REPORT

Knowledge of these developments, together with the increasing tempo of change in New Guinea, last year stimulated us to conduct a more detailed examination of the New Guinea economy. Accordingly, after consultation with the School of Pacific Studies of the Australian National University as to the scope and methods appropriate for such an inquiry, we arranged for Mr J. R. Thomas, an officer of the Bank, and Miss Dawn Ryan, an anthropologist of the University of Sydney, to carry out a survey of the sources of money income amongst the native peoples and their methods of employing and saving this income and, furthermore, to explore how far the notion of credit was understood by them and what scope there was both immediately and in the future for the extension of bank credit as a means of stimulating their economic progress.

The study was carried out on a regional basis, since it was clear

that the peoples of the different districts varied greatly in their degree
of economic development and in commercial and financial sophistica-
tion. Thus in the Gazelle Peninsula the survey showed that the indigenous population derived a substantial money income from cocoa,
copra, from sales in the native market, from stevedoring, building, hir-
ing vehicles, and conducting trade stores. The amount of this money
income was increasing rapidly as immature cacao and coconut trees
came into production. There clearly remains a substantial surplus over
consumption expenditure and only a relatively small part of this surplus flows into the various savings banks. Some is invested in such
things as improved housing and the purchase of vehicles but a good
deal continues to be hoarded.

In this area there would appear to be positive evidence of an emerging demand and justification for the provision of bank credit. One
obvious illustration is a new land settlement scheme being developed
by the Administration through one of the native local government
councils. Here a substantial area of land suitable for cocoa production
is being opened up and sub-divided into individual blocks of approximately 15 acres each. A considerable amount of clearing and other
preparatory work has to be done before planting can be undertaken
and four or five years must then elapse before the trees come into
bearing. It is contemplated that settlers will carry out this preparatory
work themselves while continuing to rely on sources within their own
village community for sustenance in the meantime. However, it would
be possible to bring this land into production more quickly if developmental work could be done in part by employed labour, but for
this to be practicable the settlers would need to be provided with
credit in relatively modest amounts. At present prices, the prospective
annual income from these blocks would be ample to service the debts
which would need to be incurred. An interesting feaure of this project
is that the land is to be allotted to the settlers on the normal Australian type leasehold tenure, which would enable it to be pledged as
security for a loan. In this respect it differs from land held under traditional native tenure under which a variety of persons have some
usage rights to the land, the system of inheritance is exceedingly complex and in any case the land cannot be mortgaged or in other ways
pledged as security.

The absence of land available as security will undoubtedly be a factor limiting the provision of credit to indigenes producing on land
held under traditional native tenure. However, it is clear that in the
Peninsula natives are beginning to ask that credit should be available to them and some of the native councils have urged that a
native people's bank should be established for this purpose. There
does not seem to be any need for the establishment of a special

institution to deal with this problem. The making of loans to agricultural producers amongst others is a normal banking function and it is not unreasonable to expect banks to adapt their security practices so that they conform to the needs and circumstances of the society in which they operate.

A further complication affecting possible loans to individuals is that at present such loans require the approval of the Administration's District Officer. The reasons for this requirement in the early stages of the people's economic development are obvious enough but it is doubtful whether it should now apply, at any rate to loans made by banks. These are unlikely to encourage an individual's indebtedness to a level endangering his independence and could be relied upon to make as effective checks of the credit-worthiness of the individual concerned as the District Officer himself.

Local government councils in this area have, apart from the Tolai cacao project, so far been able to give effect to their development plans from resources available to them without resort to credit but they are becoming progressively more ambitious and the continued success of the cacao project may well lead to further extensions of credit to local government councils for developmental purposes. Co-operatives in this area were the ones most adversely affected by the difficulties which I referred to earlier and are only recently showing signs of re-establishing themselves in the natives' eyes. As they become more effective, they could provide an additional source of demand for bank credit. There is at present some obscurity as to their legal power to borrow and give security but there would be little difficulty in having this matter clarified.

It is possible that the problem of security for loans to individuals might be overcome by some form of collective security. Thus village councils themselves, co-operatives, or perhaps specially established credit unions could become an intermediary between banks and individual borrowers. Such developments could give valuable experience and education in the conduct of credit transactions to the indigenous people themselves and might well enable more adequate judgments of credit-worthiness and more effective sanctions against persons failing to fulfil their obligations.

Clearly, the Gazelle Peninsula is the area in which the best opportunities exist for advancement in these matters. The Tolai people are efficient producers, shrewd bargainers and acquire an understanding of commercial and financial processes very quickly. The Port Moresby district presents a much more difficult and complex picture. The Moresby area is not fertile and its indigenous people have not a tradition of effective farming as have the Tolai people. A very much larger proportion of them are dependent upon income derived from employment with the Administration and with Australian owned enterprises, though income is supplemented to some extent by fishing and by the production of pottery for native trade. Because, however, of the closer association with the white community, there is a greater consciousness of the possibilities of credit and perhaps a more widespread demand for it, although it tends to be to a greater extent for housing, vehicles, outboard motors, fishing nets and the like, some of which do not greatly increase money income and consequently provide a less satisfactory basis for loans than those to finance development of agricultural production.

It is in this area that the idea of credit unions has been advanced most frequently. Such unions have been developed extensively in Fiji and some of the Moresby people are aware of them. They could perhaps form the most useful intermediary, particularly if they could be linked on the one hand with the co-operative societies which have an effective history in this area and on the other hand with the banks. In this way they could provide experience in credit matters but provide a natural line of development by which, as incomes and experience increase, members could be encouraged to establish normal banker-customer relationships with banks.

The survey also examined the position in the Morobe, Madang, Sepik and the eastern and western highlands districts, where income from native production is very much smaller and financial and commercial experience is more limited, where knowledge of and demand for credit are not important. However, conditions vary within these areas quite considerably and circumstances are changing rapidly, particularly perhaps in the eastern highlands, where some natives are beginning to earn relatively large incomes from coffee and where the number of trees coming into bearing is increasing rapidly. In this area also there is a great variety of cash crops.

The report has caused us to modify our previous generally negative impressions of the possibilities of the banking system contributing significantly to speeding up the economic and financial development of the Territories. It is clear that while conditions vary very greatly from district to district and there is need to maintain banks' traditional caution, the banking system must be prepared to modify its existing attitudes and practices to meet the rapidly changing needs of the New Guinea economy. The report has been considered in a preliminary way by all the banks represented in the area and some consultation with them has already taken place. While no firm conclusions as to future action have been reached, it is clear that banks are keen to meet the requirements of the Territory and in particular to solve the problems of providing banking services for the indigenous people. Accordingly, action is being planned to increase the effectiveness of the mobilisation of savings and to extend educational work designed to increase understanding of the benefits particularly of savings bank deposits. Secondly, there is a clear willingness to examine all reasonable propositions which might involve the extension of credit to native institutions such as councils and co-operatives and also in appropriate cases to individual natives themselves.

It is probable that the Reserve Bank, in collaboration with the Administration and others, will examine what benefits might be expected in the development of credit unions or other possible intermediaries between banks and individuals. Other banks now have under consideration the possible employment of indigenous people in banking duties and the provision of training to enable them to carry out these duties effectively. We propose to take up with the Administration possible changes in the content of the basic education provided to facilitate understanding of financial and banking matters. A more difficult problem may be the provision of supplementary education and training beyond that required for the performance of routine duties. It is this lack of general education and cultural background which may delay the advancement of indigenous clerks in the more responsible functions within the banking system.

THE RESERVE BANK IN NEW GUINEA AND THE TERRITORIES

Until recently, the Reserve Bank had not given great thought to its responsibilities in relation to the Territories independently of its general responsibilities for the Australian economy. It seems to us now, however, that we must increasingly find ways of carrying out our central banking functions for the New Guinea economy, to some extent at any rate independently of the rest of the Australian economy. We are proceeding, therefore, to build up our knowledge of the banking, financial, and general economic conditions of New Guinea independently and to seek to formulate monetary and banking policy for it along lines appropriate to its own problems. For these purposes, we will build up certain basic statistical services and carry out economic analyses which will be relevant also to the general developmental problems of the Administration and the government in the Territories. We hope, therefore, to establish close co-operation with those sections of the department and the Administration which are concerned with formulating the economic and developmental programs for the Territories. As part of this co-operation, we may be able to share in examination of major developmental projects which may arise from developmental plans and carry out studies of the economics of particular forms of production, particularly those forming part of the productive economy of the indigenous people.

It will, of course, be the responsibility of the Reserve Bank to watch the effectiveness of the adaptation of the banking system itself to the emerging needs of the economy of the Territories and to ensure that this adaptation is adequate and effective. We will need to study also the development of the subsidiary financial institutions among the indigenous people and their relationship with the banking system proper.

From the resources available to it, the Bank may also be able to sponsor the basic study of some of the fundamental problems of the Territories. It appears to us urgent, for instance, that the problem of protein deficiency in the diet of many of the indigenous people should be further explored and possible ways of supplementing their diet from forms of production possible within their resources and knowledge be tested in practice. We believe also that the signs of the emergence of a landless proletariat around the administrative centres calls for urgent study of the sources of income available to these people, their adequacy and methods by which they can be supplemented. The study of these and other similar problems is a matter on which the Bank is anxious to seek the advice of CSIRO, the Australian National University, international institutions, as well as others competent to advise it.

Apart from these immediate problems facing the Reserve Bank, there is one fundamental and exceedingly difficult problem which concerns us. It is clearly the intention of the government that Australian policies should be based on the expectation that in due course complete self-government will be given to the indigenous people of New Guinea. When such self-government is given, it may well be possible for commercial banks operating in the area to continue, provided of course they have in the meantime served the needs of the community adequately. The coming of independence would, however, almost certainly mean that the new nation would need to establish its own central bank. At any rate our work should be based upon this expectation. It is therefore part of the responsibility of the Reserve Bank to plan and develop within its own organisation sections dealing with the problems of the Territories into which members of the indigenous peoples are drawn increasingly for training, experience and responsibility. To have ready within the sort of period which might be available before independence is sought even the nucleus of an effective central banking organisation, equipped and staffed with persons drawn from the New Guinea communities, is clearly a task of frightening complexity and difficulty, particularly in the light of the educational standards so far achieved within the Territories themselves. However, neither the complexity nor the difficulty of the task reduces its urgency. Accordingly, the Bank proposes to make an immediate start on the development of this New Guinea nucleus within its own organisation.

The Reserve Bank
in Papua-New Guinea

I ASSUME, in this paper, that there is a firm and continuing transfer of political power to the indigenous people, the residents of New Guinea. I assume that it is the Australian Government's intention, an intention endorsed by the Australian people generally, to try to keep ahead of the demands of the local people in this transfer of power so that at all times we are trying to do a little less in the way of managing New Guinea affairs than perhaps the majority of indigenous people would wish.

I would like to comment that to me there seems grave danger in the transfer of political power not accompanied by the transfer and acceptance of responsibility. Anybody who listened to the clear and eloquent statement by the member for Milne Bay, Mr John Guise, would have been struck by the awareness the local members in the House of Assembly have of their functions as representatives of their electorate and of the pressure to which they are subject to seek things which their constituents want. There is danger in a situation in which it is easy for constituents to express wants and for representatives to demand that they be satisfied without either being forced to consider their practicability or cost.

The realities of political power are brought together in the budget. This is the focus of political decision. Whoever determines the pattern of the budget exercises the essence of political power. Accordingly, those people who are considering the constitutional development of Papua and New Guinea should face the question of how soon it will be possible to transfer the making and approving of the budget to the local people. So long as Australia provides a large proportion of the aggregate expenditure in the budget, this is going to be difficult. Nevertheless, I wonder whether it might not be possible to identify Australian financial support for the New Guinea budget with certain sections of that budget, leaving certain specific functions, particularly those most closely identified with the day-to-day life of the people and embodying

Paper to the Council on New Guinea Affairs, Goroka, 14 April 1965. Reproduced by permission of *New Guinea*.

their most immediate ambitions and desires, to be financed from revenue raised in Papua and New Guinea. For instance, several indigenous speakers in this seminar have referred to the passionate desire for more extensive educational facilities and for a continuation and improvement of health facilities. These are two things—education at any rate at the primary level—which the World Bank Report suggested might perhaps be steadied off and greater priority given to other objectives.

Now, it is natural and understandable that the New Guinea people should value these services highly—as indeed I do myself. Nevertheless, it might be a salutary exercise if at an early stage the House of Assembly should be given effective responsibility for them and their financing. They would then have to consider how extensions of these services were to be financed, or what priority they should be given over alternative claims on the proceeds of local revenue. They may have to decide to forgo them or some other desirable improvement or to accept higher taxes. This would face them with one of the facts of life of political independence. At the outset, the area of their direct responsibility would be limited but sufficient to give them valuable experience. Progressively, too, it suggests a procedure for gradual transfer of decision making. Australian aid could be progressively limited to a narrow range of purposes—perhaps in the not too distant future to capital development and special services such as tertiary education. Ultimately, even these might be financed on a loan basis. In this way, transfer of political power could carry effective executive responsibility within appropriate but steadily widening limits.

I make these comments to draw attention to what seems to me to be a dangerous tendency to imagine that it is possible to achieve development, higher standards of living and increasing public services without significant cost and, indeed, without people having to go without anything or sacrifice anything to get them. In a brief statement this morning the indigenous representative from Bougainville, Mr Paul Lapun, more than any other speaker, faced the issue that, if the people of New Guinea want things, they must be prepared to contribute something towards them. There seems also a dangerous tendency to imagine that foreign aid from countries other than Australia is potentially very large. We may legitimately be criticised for failure to use all the possible international facilities, but to imagine that such facilities could make a significant difference to the burden of finding and financing the physical and human resources for New Guinea development would be to delude ourselves and the people of New Guinea.

I would like also to comment generally on the Report of the I.B.R.D. and how we should approach it. The Report was, I think, quite clearly intended to provide a program of action designed to expedite economic development in New Guinea. It is true that the report does not make clear how far the program of action proposed would contribute to or be consistent with the economic viability of New Guinea or expedite political reform and the movement towards political independence. In fairness to the World Bank Mission it seems to me it should be judged by its usefulness in suggesting to the Australian Government and to the Administration of Papua and New Guinea what would be the highest priority tasks in the enormous job of raising the standards of production and of real incomes among the peoples of these territories.

My main dissatisfaction with the Report arose from a lack of precision in dealing with the task of stimulating indigenous enterprise. The Mission saw European activity as a catalyst, something which, given opportunity at key points in the economy, would stimulate parallel activity among the indigenous peoples. There is justification for this view but I would have been happier if it had been made clearer how this catalytic effect was to occur and what institutional and other developments would make it more likely. However, since they have in the main left this problem, it seems appropriate that in this paper I should devote my attention to examining what is being done in the Reserve Bank and how far it will help stimulate indigenous activity—in parallel with the European activity for which the World Bank has set out reasonable blueprints.

Before doing this, it may be necessary to say a little about the functions of a reserve bank. A reserve bank issues and distributes the legal currency, particularly the note issue, as it is required in the community and it acts as banker to the government, to other banks, and in some cases to other financial institutions, serving these much in the same way as commercial banks serve businesses or members of the community. Further, it seeks to regulate the use of credit so that it contributes effectively to development and to the maintenance of reasonable stability within the economy as a whole.

These functions and the means whereby they are carried out are fairly clearly understood in well-developed economies. But in a country such as New Guinea the financial system is not much more than embryonic. So far as the indigenous part of the community is concerned, awareness of money and its functions in economic affairs is limited. There are still extensive areas of New Guinea and Papua which are essentially still non-money economies, although with the development of cash crops and working for wages the role of money is steadily increasing. But it still must be borne in mind that we are talking about an economy in transition from a non-money to a money economy. Consequently, if credit and the financial system are to perform their functions effectively, the first task is to develop financial institutions serving the indigenous people, creating those institutions where they do not yet exist, developing them where they exist in embryonic form and guiding their development so that they contribute best to the development of the economy as a whole and to the welfare of the indigenous people.

Creating, developing and guiding an emerging financial system is a complex task in which we can get little guidance from the experience of other peoples. It seems to us, however, that there are three aspects of this task:

(1) To educate the indigenous people in the significance of money and in the working of an economy based on money.

(2) To bring the indigenous people themselves into financial institutions at the grass-roots level—institutions which they themselves will use, will develop and, so far as practicable, will manage for themselves.

(3) To lead them gradually to participation in and the use of more sophisticated financial institutions which have been introduced from abroad—the banking system proper, corporations and the capital market generally.

I would like now to refer briefly, but concretely, to action we have taken over the last three years and to indicate the way in which we hope this will proceed. My references may seem pedestrian and concerned with detail but it may be helpful to this conference to look at the issues which concern a particular institution like the Reserve Bank, in carrying out its responsibilities in these territories. Also in this way we may benefit from the criticism and suggestions you may have to offer.

The task of financial education requires both some knowledge about money and some practice in working with it. It is necessary to establish the connections in a money economy between work, money, and expenditure; between borrowing, using, and repaying. These are to us commonplace ideas which form part of the pattern of society. But they are novel to many of the New Guinea communities before these have been influenced by European ways, although we should not ignore the fact that notions of commerce, wealth, and associated prestige have deep roots among some of them. This kind of knowledge is important not merely in economic life but also in the political development of the community. Without it, how can the electorate judge the appropriateness of the plans which are put before them? How can they judge the wisdom or capacity of the people who offer themselves as their representatives, a large part of whose work is going to be concerned with the control and management of public expenditure or of particular forms of public expenditure?

Progress in the understanding of money has been stimulated by cash crops which require production for and dealing in the market. Cash cropping in the last decade has caused a fivefold increase in the money incomes of indigenous peoples. From this source, their holdings in savings bank balances and other money holdings have increased by something like four times. It is clear that the money economy is on the way. But to develop it further and more rapidly we have been conducting an educational program for the native peoples through booklets and films in which the basic ideas are set forth in relatively simple terms. Booklets have been circulated which deal with:

(1) the forms and functions of money;
(2) wealth—what it is and how it is obtained;
(3) the functions and purposes of a market, how prices are determined in it and how changes in prices can serve as a guide to their efforts;
(4) banks and banking;
(5) keeping a cheque account.

These are things which indigenous people, as they come to share in commercial activities, will need to understand. These booklets in various languages are circulated, in the first instance through post-primary schools, to teachers and to trainee teachers, through co-operatives, through agricultural extension workers and others who come into daily contact with people who are developing their economic activities in the market. We are beginning to follow up these booklets with films which present visually the ideas set out in the booklets. It is hard to judge how effective this campaign of education is but we feel sufficiently encouraged to continue.

In this activity, the Reserve Bank is associated with all the Australian banks operating in New Guinea, which give their full support to this and other aspects of the education and development of the indigenous people in the financial field.

The next phase of our program is the development of indigenous financial institutions—what might be called a sub-banking system or a banking system at the grass-roots level. In essence, a bank is a simple institution. It is an intermediary between two sets of people—those who are saving from their incomes or who have accumulated idle money balances and those people who wish to spend more than their income or who lack sufficient money balances to finance their expenditure. One set has a surplus to lend, the other has a need to borrow. A bank is an institution which stands between these two groups and acts as an intermediary so that those who need to use the savings or the idle balances can borrow them without having to run around to find what lucky man has a surplus. It is therefore quite possible to conceive and establish a bank on a very small scale. In a way we have been doing this in the establishment of what we call the Savings and Loan Societies. These societies are conducted by the indigenes working together, going to the same church or being in some way associated, who combine to save regularly and pool their savings. The savings can then be used by the group to deposit with a bank, to invest, or especially to lend to members of the group for suitable purposes. Such Savings and Loan Societies, established throughout the Territory, will serve both as mobilisers of indigenous saving and, more particularly, as sources of small loans for the economic advancement of the indigenous people. More generally, they are a practical instrument by which people can learn what credit is, how it works, how you use it, and above all how you manage it. Each of these societies is conducted by the indigenous members. A Reserve Bank officer acts, by arrangement with the Administration, as the Registrar of these Societies. We have offices in Moresby and Rabaul, in Lae, in Goroka, and in Mt Hagen, and will, in due course, have offices to promote their development in all parts of the Territory. The functions of the Bank as Registrar are to explain to groups of the indigenous people what these societies are and how they can be helpful to them; to help set them up; to train their officers, and generally to watch their progress.

The society proceeds to full activity by two steps. In the first, the society is just a savings club—a group of people who agree to save at a regular rate and to pool their savings. In this stage the proceeds are placed in a bank or invested in securities issued by the Administration. When we are satisfied that the group is effective and its management is capable of conducting the affairs of the society, it can become a Savings and Loan Society and can make loans to its members. Usually a year's experience is necessary before this second stage is reached. It is interesting to note that in some communities it has not been easy to develop the idea of loans to members. Understanding of the purposes for which it is good sense to borrow emerges slowly even when the societies are in a position to make loans.

You might be interested in the results that have been achieved during the three years in which the Reserve Bank, in collaboration with the Administration and the trading banks, has been working on these societies. We now have 260 separate groups, of which 44 have become full Savings and Loan Societies. These cover 12,000 members and have accumulated total funds of £117,000. These funds have come partly from the proceeds of cash crops and partly from wages earned by their members. The funds, the £117,000, are at present used in the following way—some £93,000 is held in bank balances, £12,000 in investments, almost entirely in the securities of the Administration, and £12,000 is now out on loans to members. Among the groups which have become full Loan Societies, 60 per cent of the funds are still in bank balances and the remainder is divided evenly—20 per cent in investments and 20 per cent in loans to members, but the ratio of loans has been for some time fairly steadily rising. In a few, but only a few, societies loans to members are becoming the most important use of their funds.

Loans have been made for clearing land, for planting cash crops, for buying copra dryers, fencing wire, home building materials, tools of trade, motor vehicles (usually to groups of people), bicycles, sewing machines, and an interesting one—for the payment of educational expenses. These examples indicate that, although lending by these societies has gone slowly, there is evidence that the people of New Guinea are able to decide for what kinds of purpose credit can be effectively used.

Loans have been made in amounts as small as £5 and as large as £100, which is the maximum to one person, and so far the members appear to understand and to accept the obligations for repayment and for the payment of interest. So far no significant difficulty has been experienced in collecting instalments from borrowers. Already, with £12,000 of loans outstanding, repayments have been made totalling £4,000.

How important can these societies become? There is some evidence that they could quickly become significant. In the Gazelle Peninsula within three years one in five of the total male and female adult population is a member of one of these societies. Progress in the other districts has been slower but very promising—especially where cash incomes are growing. Groups of societies can federate and it seems likely that this will occur on a regional basis. This could lead to more effective use of the societies' funds and to a spreading of risks because some societies tend to have a greater capacity to accumulate savings than to lend them among their own members.

It is possible that the societies could become a useful means of channelling credit from other sources. Supervision of the borrowing is undertaken by the members themselves who can be expected to watch carefully over their own money. Further, it is easier for them to discipline reluctant payers than it would be for a bank. This has educational value as well as helping the stability of the society. It is worth while considering whether banks and any development finance corporation might not make loans to the societies for retailing to their members.

While these societies should remain essentially indigenous, we hope they will develop an increasing association with the banking system. All banks which operate in the Territories have co-operated with the Reserve Bank in their development. Both Reserve Bank officers and officers seconded by the commercial banks help with the work of developing and supervising the societies. This establishes between individual banks and individual societies a family relationship as a result of which the bank watches over the welfare of a particular society without seeking to interfere in the conduct of its affairs but with sufficient concern to be able to utter a warning if this appears necessary. Furthermore, the indigenous people, gradually becoming more experienced in financial affairs while remaining members of their Savings and Loan Society, will naturally tend to become customers of commercial banks with greater ease and comprehension of the benefits of such a relationship. In this way the more sophisticated institutions, coming into this country in the first instance mainly for the use of the European settlers and businessmen, will progressively acquire an indigenous character.

I want to touch very briefly on the question which is raised prominently in the World Bank Report but which has not received attention in this seminar; that is the provision for development finance. The World Bank Report recommended that there should be a single corporation set up partly with private and partly with public funds. It would not be appropriate for me to comment in detail but there are one or two points which I would like to touch on. First, credit is not something which can be used without limit. Even if the sources of credit can be established, there are physical limits to its effective use —limits sometimes of manpower or of special skills, sometimes of physical resources, sometimes limitations of equipment, buildings and other capital equipment and, above all, of managerial and entre-preneurial skill. These things may well set more stringent limits to what can be achieved than those set by credit. One cannot assume merely because money can be found to satisfy the demands of borrowers that this will lead automatically to development.

However, coming to the ways in which the development finance should be provided, it is worth recalling that needs for development finance are diverse in amount and purpose. Demands will come from large corporations and from the humble indigenous farmer to clear a little land or plant a few trees. It would not be easy for the same institution effectively to meet all these demands. While a large-scale development finance corporation of the kind envisaged by the World Bank is almost certainly necessary, I believe it is important also that existing financial institutions, and perhaps particularly banks, should recognise that they have a responsibility to participate at appropriate levels. As I have mentioned, at the levels of small-scale finance the Savings and Loan Societies themselves may be able to contribute.

Development finance can be the function of a variety of institutions, some already in existence. If banks are going to operate effectively in this field they will have to be ingenious. Australian banks in the past have shown a considerable degree of imagination in finding ways around the hidebound rules of thumb sometimes followed by their European forebears. If they have had a client in whom and in whose enterprise they had confidence, they usually found a way of overcoming security difficulties and enabling the client to be given reasonable credit. It would be very helpful if the Australian banks operating in New Guinea were to exercise similar ingenuity.

I want to touch finally on the staffing of the financial system. Political independence will mean little unless the indigenous people develop administrative and executive independence too—that is learn to conduct their affairs at all levels. This applies not merely to government administration but also to the conduct of the business and financial institutions. Indigenous people should be educated and trained to accept increasing responsibility in these institutions including the banking system. The trading banks and ourselves have over some years made a small start in the employment of indigenes. Success has been limited and we now face some uncertainty about going further. This is not necessarily due to a deficiency in the staff themselves. It is easy to bring an indigenous officer into a bank and to allow him to perform the rather routine functions which usually engage the energies of young bank officers, but if he is going to go beyond that an act of faith is called for—the bank must be prepared to trust the officer with decisions which in the past have been entrusted only to a European. There is a gap here which still has to be bridged. Part of the difficulty comes, I think, from the attitude of the European community in the Territory. It will not be possible for a bank to perform the act of faith required unless its clients are prepared to accept it. No bank can offend the clients on whom it depends. If there is a sense of constraint between the clients of the bank and indigenous employees which inhibits the employee in performing his task, an almost impossible decision faces the bank itself. It has been said in this conference that we should work on the assumption that there is no task in the Territory which could not in due course be performed by an indigene. This I accept and I believe we have reached a stage in the banking system where we must act on this assumption. However, the banks may need to be helped in this matter.

At this stage, it may be helpful if officers who are showing promise could have a short period of supplementary training in which they learnt more about the banks as an institution and the way in which they function. This could help them acquire more confidence in their dealings with clients. It will be necessary, too, to provide additional educational background at the point of recruitment so the indigenes entering the bank can acquire greater understanding of the institutional background which can be assumed in European recruits. Perhaps the Reserve Bank and the trading banks could work in association to bridge these gaps.

In the Reserve Bank we believe that we must push on with the employment of indigenes at various levels. We are, therefore, planning considerable progress over the next few years. Already, of the twenty-six male staff working in the Territory, eleven are indigenous. By the end of the year we hope that the proportion will have risen to about 60 per cent. Within three or four years almost all the positions, except those associated at this stage with higher management, will, we hope, be staffed by indigenes. It should not be long before we are able to dispense altogether with female staff from outside the Territory. Senior positions present some difficulty since the functions of the Bank are complex and call for an understanding of matters beyond the present experience of most indigenes. It requires time Professor Sayers, Professor of Banking and Economics in the University of London, has said: 'If there are to be effective central bankers tomorrow, there must be young men growing up in central banks, soaking themselves in the traditions and techniques of central banking'.

It is, of course, not merely a question of absorbing the past. Merely to do that would be a disaster. Every society must develop its own central bank, having its roots in the financial system and traditions of that society. It must develop its own techniques. It can learn from other banks, but cannot take over their methods mechanically.

We must find young men of ability, see that they get the education, the opportunities to learn from us and from other parts of the world but, at the same time, see that they apply these lessons in New Guinea with a real understanding of the character and purposes of their own society. We have made a small start in this. We have at the present time three students working in the University of Sydney on Bank bursaries. One of these, we hope, will graduate this year. The others should not be long thereafter. We have other officers at lower stages in the educational ladder and we intend to maintain this program. As the tertiary institutions in the Territory develop, we hope to use them effectively. Within a few years, we expect to have a small group of intelligent and dedicated New Guineans and Papuans who have been given both opportunity and responsibility. There are risks in this but I believe we shall make more mistakes by being reluctant to entrust responsibility than we shall if we accept the risks. However, inevitably there will be some mistakes. Indeed, mistakes are an essential part of the process of learning. And above all, these mistakes will be a small price to pay for effective progress in identifying the financial institutions of New Guinea and Papua with the people they are being designed to serve.

PART II

*Internal Balance,
External Balance,
and Growth*

Economic Development
and Financial Stability

As I see the function of this address, it is to survey in broad outline the nature of the relationship between economic development and financial stability as it appears to the general practitioner in the economic field. By doing so I hope to provide a general background which will throw into bolder relief the relevance of the analysis of the economic specialists to the more immediate problems of our economy.

DEFINITIONS

Let me first make clear the sense in which I propose to use these terms. By economic development I mean the use of resources, both human and material, to increase our capacity to produce goods and services—in other words, action by which we can increase and improve our equipment, technique, and skills. Economic development is one way of using our resources, and to use them for this purpose means of course that they cannot be used for others. Thus resources can be used to produce:

(1) goods and services for current consumption such as food, clothing, medical attention, maintenance of law and order;

(2) consumers' equipment such as refrigerators, motor cars, radios, houses;

(3) social equipment such as schools, hospitals, administrative buildings;

(4) producers' equipment which includes collective property such as railways, roads, and power plants, and corporate property such as factories, shops and offices, as well as individually owned equipment such as farm improvements, tools of trade and the like.

Narrowly defined, economic development should perhaps mean the use of resources to produce goods in the last category, but in Australia economic development is associated with and to some extent identified

Presidential Address, Section G, ANZAAS, Melbourne, August 1955. Reproduced by permission of *Economic Record* and the *Australian Journal of Science*.

with increasing population, and it is, therefore, appropriate to include those forms of equipment, particularly social equipment and houses, that are necessary to equip an increasing population.

Financial stability must be looked at in two ways. Internally I take it to mean the absence of substantial change in the value of money. If the Australian pound continues over the years to buy approximately the same quantities of goods and services of the kind people normally spend their money on, it can be regarded as stable. Absolute stability in this sense is impossible if only because the complex of goods in which people are interested changes, but the concept is clear enough for practical purposes. From the external point of view the concept of financial stability is different. In a world of freely moving exchange rates it could perhaps be identified with reasonable stability in such rates, but, in a world where variation in exchange rates occurs rarely and then only in response to a fundamental change in international economic relations, another criterion must be sought. When a country is facing difficulty in its international payments, it is now almost normal practice for its government to take action through exchange control and import restrictions to limit the effects of these difficulties and in a practical sense the existence, the severity, and the persistence of such controls can be regarded as evidence of some measure of departure from external stability. In extreme cases of instability these measures may prove inadequate and a variation of exchange rates themselves may occur. This concept is even less precise than that of internal financial stability and is different in kind since it is affected directly by what is happening in other countries. It should be noted that the two types of stability need not run together. A country could be experiencing internal financial stability at the same time as it experienced instability in its external financial relations, and vice versa.

In other words a country can be regarded as enjoying financial stability if, over the period concerned, its domestic currency purchases an approximately uniform quantity of goods and services of the kind desired and if its nationals can spend or make payments abroad without significant restraint.

PRESUMPTIONS

It is clear that most people would regard economic development and financial stability in the sense we have used them as desirable, and certainly they are very much in the minds of most Australians from time to time. It is the purpose of this paper to explore the broad relationships between them—to see how the pursuit of economic development may influence financial stability and to draw such conclusions as may be practicable about how we can best achieve them both.

It is important in an examination of this kind to be clear about the presumptions which underlie our approach. For instance, the issues would present a different picture to a person who thought economic development a waste of effort or to one who enjoyed fishing in the troubled waters of financial instability. For the purpose of this paper I have, therefore, accepted the following broad presumptions, believing them to express a kind of common denominator of Australian contemporary attitudes:

(1) That economic development is desirable both as a means to full employment and higher standards of living and as an end in itself.

(2) That it is desirable that the value of money within the economy should be stable through time although minor variations are not of great significance.

(3) That it is desirable that Australians should be free to buy, to travel, and to make payments abroad within the limits of their own resources, but that this end should not be pursued to the extent that it seriously endangers reasonable economic development, full employment, or reasonable internal stability in the value of money.

(4) That, within some limits, it is legitimate for governments to take action designed to increase the proportion of the economy's resources devoted to economic development beyond what it would be if left to individual decisions.

(5) That if financial stability is endangered, it is legitimate for a government to take action directly or indirectly to preserve it.

(6) That action by government necessary for these purposes should operate as far as possible on the factors determining the general economic and financial climate so that the decisions of individuals and enterprises are freely made in the light of apparently objective considerations.

It should, of course, be observed that these desiderata may be partially in conflict and that practical decisions will require a balancing of one against the other.

RESOURCES FOR DEVELOPMENT

Since economic development is a form of production, it follows that the resources available for it are the resources available for production of all kinds—the labour, natural resources, equipment, and skills of the country and its people. These resources can be used directly or indirectly, that is, they can be used to produce the goods and services finally required by the community or they can be used to produce exports which are exchanged abroad for imports of goods and services finally needed. The possible total volume of goods and services available within the economy depends partly on our own productive capacity, but partly also on the terms of trade—the bases on which we can exchange exports for imports. This is a very important factor to Australia. Since the war wool has exchanged on the average for $1\frac{1}{2}$ times as many imports as it did in the five years before the war. This has added substantially both to our standards of consumption and to our rate of development.

First claim on these resources is made by expenditure on goods and services for immediate consumption purchased individually and those provided and paid for by public authorities. To these must be added expenditure on consumers' equipment which in the contemporary scene is making increasing claims on the resources of the economy. It is only to the extent that resources are freed for other purposes by saving—by abstaining from making claims on resources for consumption—that expenditure on development is possible without excessive pressure on available resources. What is the position in Australia?

We used to think that if there was one thing we really knew about the working of the economy it was the stability of the relation between consumption and income. The events of the last ten years, both in Australia and in other countries, have rather shaken our confidence.

The percentage of income spent on consumer goods and services has fallen as incomes have increased, although there appears to have been a reversal of this tendency in the last couple of years. During the 1930s personal consumption absorbed about 75 per cent of the supplies available after deducting movements in stocks; in the last five years the percentage has been between 60 and 65. This fall has been partly attributable to an increase in the proportion of income absorbed by taxation and has been accompanied by an increase in government expenditure of a current nature, particularly on defence. Current government expenditure now absorbs about 10 per cent of available supplies compared with less than 6 per cent pre-war. However, even allowing for this increase in government expenditure, the proportion of resources available for development has increased significantly, from about 20 per cent in the late 1930s to over 26 per cent in the last five years.

What is the likely trend of consumption expenditure in the near future? Consumption standards will presumably continue to rise with incomes, but it is not clear how the proportion of consumption to income will change. Although there is some reason to expect that the proportion of income saved will increase as incomes rise, new products and new tastes, the wider use of hire purchase credit, and continued economic security might well encourage consumers to spend a constant or even increasing proportion of their incomes.

The resources left for development in the Australian economy, after consumption needs have been met, have been maintained within recent years at relatively high levels. Indeed, Australia ranks among the group of countries with the highest rates of development.

From what has been said it can be seen:

(1) that development is a form of production and is an alternative to production for other purposes;

(2) that the various forms of production are initiated by expenditure and that the allocation of resources between them is determined by the allocation of expenditure by individuals, by business, by public authorities and by governments.

The significance of expenditure in this process suggests a nexus between economic development and financial stability at least in its internal aspect. Let us follow it through step by step.

RELATIONSHIP BETWEEN EXPENDITURE, PRODUCTION, EMPLOYMENT, AND PRICES

The resources available from the total for development are limited to those not used to produce consumption goods and services, and this quantity is determined (unless there are labour and other resources being left idle) by what people, firms, and governments save from their incomes.

Decisions to spend on development are generally made independently of decisions to save; consequently, there is no reason why the resources required to give effect to the decisions to spend on development should prove to be equal to those which are made available by decisions to save.

It can happen, therefore, that the decisions to spend on consumption on the one hand and on development on the other can in the aggregate be more than or less than the amount that could be satisfied from current production at current prices.

If there is a tendency for spending to run beyond the value of current production, the effect is felt first on the stocks of goods held which are reduced by the extra spending. This in itself encourages attempts to increase production, and firms seek to increase the labour and other resources they employ. If the economy is already fully employed, their attempts to do so bid up the prices of labour and materials with consequent rises in the costs of production. These rises in costs can generally be passed on readily in increased prices when demand is at a high level. Furthermore, shortages tend to appear because demand exceeds supplies and competition tends to force up prices generally. Thus in a situation where decisions to spend on consumption and on development would involve the use of more labour and materials than are available at current prices there appear shortages, rising costs, and rising prices.

On the other hand, if there is a tendency for spending to be less than the value of potential current production at current prices, the impact is felt first by stocks of goods which accumulate unsold in the hands of merchants and producers. This in itself leads to decisions to reduce production, leading to unemployment and waste of resources. Surplus stocks lead to cutting of prices, and unemployment to wage cutting and reductions in incomes, which lead in turn to lower costs and prices.

These two processes tend to be cumulative so that both overspending and underspending are inclined to be intensified by the results they produce. Thus, overspending produces rising costs and prices, with resultant increases in profits and other incomes which make expansion appear attractive and so intensify the tendency for spending to be increased. On the other hand, underspending produces unemployment with loss of income which means that spending will be cut further and the incentive to spend on development correspondingly reduced.

In the depression period of 1930–5 we had a classic illustration of a period of underspending. The drive for development had apparently spent itself during the 1920s and there seemed a dearth of opportunities. Unemployment on a widespread and intensive scale was normal and there was continual downward pressure on wages and other incomes.

The period from 1945–51 presents the opposite picture. The wartime accumulation of arrears of capital replacement, stimulated by increasing population and the emergence of new opportunities for industrial growth, produced a flood of plans for expenditure on development—by governments, firms, and individuals. This expenditure quickly outran possible production and we experienced the familiar cycle of shortages, rising costs, rising prices following one another in increasing tempo. During this period the internal value of the Australian pound was seriously unstable—so much so that in the later stages confidence in its future was gravely impaired, to the extent that many people were unwilling to hold assets in fixed money form, for example, in government securities, and sought forms of assets such as land and equity shares whose prices might be expected to move with changing money values. This unwillingness to hold wealth in the form of money, by increasing the demand for property and shares, intensified the rise in prices and the urge to expansion. Furthermore, in this period we had a taste of the social inequities caused by a rapid deterioration in the value of money which created hardship for pensioners and others on fixed incomes and wiped out much of the value of past savings.

This period of inflation was ended in 1951/52 by a sharp fall in our export income, and a flood of imported goods. These produced an acute financial stringency and a buyers' market for goods as a result of which there was a widespread revision of developmental plans, public and private, to a scale more nearly within our physical capacity.

Thus, it can be seen that expenditure on development as a major and variable component of total expenditure can affect profoundly internal financial stability. Unless this expenditure is sufficient, together with expenditure on consumption, to employ fully our labour and resources, we are likely to experience falling prices and incomes with a cumulative tendency to unemployment and depression in the economy. On the other hand, once expenditure on development passes the point at which, together with expenditure on consumption, it is adequate to employ our resources fully, we are likely to experience rising prices, shortages, and waste characteristic of periods of inflation.

RELATIONSHIP BETWEEN DEVELOPMENT AND EXTERNAL STABILITY

The relationship between spending on development and external financial stability is less immediately apparent but is just as important.

It is easy to see that in any significant amount of expenditure in Australia there will be involved some expenditure overseas—if not on the goods or services themselves then on raw materials, capital equipment, interest or profits, royalties, and so on. Therefore, the higher the level of expenditure in Australia, the greater the amount of overseas expenditure involved. Expenditure on consumer goods and services of imported origin has a direct and corresponding effect on overseas expenditure: expenditure on consumer goods locally produced usually requires expenditure on imported materials and equipment to an extent that varies according to the nature of the goods. Expenditure on development frequently involves imports of equipment, materials, and so on, as well as payments of royalties and other similar charges.

It is important to note that once full employment has been reached, further increases in expenditure on any types of goods tend to result in almost corresponding increases in expenditure abroad. Since production here cannot be increased, suppliers turn to imports for additional supplies. Thus at times of high expenditure it is normal to see in our import statistics substantial sums in payment for commodities in which Australia might reasonably be expected to be self-sufficient.

We see then that there is a direct relationship between the levels of expenditure in Australia and the demand for imported goods and services. What are the resources from which this demand can be satisfied? Each year we sell abroad a substantial volume of exports which gives us an international income and enables us to spend abroad. The amount of this income depends on the volume of our export production and the prices the exports command, while the amount of imports we can buy from this income depends on the cost of imported goods. Our capacity to buy imports depends, therefore, basically upon the scale and efficiency of our export industries and the terms of trade on which we exchange their products for imports—the relationship between export and import prices.

This basic income can be supplemented by the proceeds of overseas borrowing and the investment by non-Australians of funds in Australia and also by the extent to which we draw on our international reserves. Money lent to or invested in Australia, for whatever purpose the money is initially spent in Australia, adds to the flow of foreign currency available, and thus enables Australia as a whole to purchase correspondingly more imports. Similarly, if we have reserves of gold and other international currencies and are prepared to draw upon them, we can buy more imports than our current export income will purchase. But it is important to remember that international reserves must be accumulated by refraining from spending export income or the proceeds of borrowing and that they can be spent only once.

Consequently, we see that there are definite limits to our capacity to pay for imports—limits set by our production of exports, by the terms on which we exchange exports for imports, by the amount we are able to borrow abroad, and by the size of our international reserves and our willingness to run them down. But our propensity to spend on imports is dependent primarily upon general levels of spending in Australia—levels which at least in the short run are to a large extent independent of our capacity to pay for imports.

It is, therefore, possible that spending in Australia on consumption and on development can rise to levels that exceed our capacity to pay for the imports needed to make that spending effective. In such a situation the first effect is for reserves to be drawn upon to finance the excess imports. If the excess is temporary, or is checked naturally or by internal measures of policy, the drain on reserves may be halted and perhaps reversed, but there is no fully effective automatic tendency to bring about this reversal. Indeed, a cumulative inflationary process can easily maintain internal spending at levels that continue progressively to deplete international reserves. In such circumstances, if the inflationary process is not halted, it will become impossible to provide the foreign currencies necessary for the payment of imports at their current price and import restrictions and exchange controls will have to be applied or intensified.

On the other hand, if the internal levels of expenditure are low enough for the demand for imports to be insufficient to use the international resources becoming available, international reserves could accumulate possibly even to a point where it would appear that the country is being deprived of some of the benefits of its current international prosperity.

Does this mean that, if we can so control our domestic expenditure that we just maintain the full employment of our labour and other internal resources, our expenditure on imports will neatly balance our income from exports and overseas borrowing? Not necessarily. Whether we can pay for the imports required by the level of expenditure associated with full employment depends upon our capacity to produce for export and the terms of trade on which we can exchange exports for imports. Largely this is a question of the relationship between internal and external costs—but not entirely. Export industry, particularly if it is agricultural or pastoral, may have a considerable potential for expansion at existing cost ratios, but to make that potential effective may require considerable capital expenditure, time for improvements to become mature, and possibly even structural changes such as subdivision of land. These may delay the achievement of international balance under the pressure of high expenditure even if cost ratios are satisfactory. But excessive expenditure associated with over-full employment is bound to put pressure on the international balance in all but the most exceptionally favourable conditions for the relative prices of exports and imports. Furthermore, a sudden deterioration in the terms of trade may create conditions in which it is impossible to preserve both full employment and an international balance except at a lower level of internal costs.

It is clear, therefore, that, if it were necessary to maintain strictly at all times conditions of external financial stability, it would be an exceedingly complex and difficult task, requiring as it would both an appropriate level of internal expenditure and a level of internal costs properly adjusted to a continuously changing relationship between export and import prices.

Fortunately it is possible to build a buffer between the internal economy and the frequent changes in the factors affecting our international balance of payments. We protect ourselves by the maintenance of international monetary reserves which we allow to fluctuate widely. By so doing we are able to ignore minor and passing influences and to give ourselves time to adjust to more persistent and fundamental changes. But this technique assumes that the pressures on our balance of payments will be sometimes one way and sometimes another. If we fail to bring under control a lack of balance in internal expenditure or to adjust ourselves to fundamental changes in our terms of trade, we can reach a position where we can no longer accept the consequential changes in the amount of our reserves and import restrictions and exchange controls of increasing severity become inevitable.

Fluctuations in the Australian balance of payments are very large by comparison with those of many other countries, and since the 1930s, therefore, we have come to regard occasional resort to import restrictions and exchange control as almost normal techniques of economic management. They can be very effective in bringing under control expenditure abroad and without doubt they are a useful addition to the techniques available to us. Even more than the use of reserves, however, they have no effect on the causes of the difficulties. The demand for imports arises out of expenditure in Australia and to prevent that demand becoming effective does not reduce the levels of expenditure but tends merely to concentrate it on domestic resources. Furthermore, by this concentration import restrictions will encourage those who are planning further development. But, if domestic resources are already being used to capacity, the imposition of import restrictions by themselves will intensify the internal pressure and render internal financial instability more probable.

The importance of the international balance of payments in relation to development is well illustrated by our changing experience since the war when we have shown a persistent propensity to spend on development. This arose partly from arrears of development caused by the war but was greatly stimulated by the relative cost advantage enjoyed by Australia as a result of its wartime control of prices. Since then the steady and rapid increase in population, creating as it does both the need for equipment of great variety and also the market opportunities for new classes of industry, together with technical change in primary and manufacturing industries, has provided a positive urge for developmental expenditure.

At this time our international position was exceptionally strong. Our relative costs were low and our exports were commanding scarcity prices. Furthermore, we had built up and were still adding to very substantial reserves of international currencies. In these circumstances we were able to proceed boldly with expenditure on development without being conscious of the limits that can be imposed by the balance of payments. Gradually, however, the special advantages of our immediate post-war situation have been reduced as international trade conditions became progressively more normal. Our cost structure gradually rose as price controls were relaxed and continued to rise under the pressure of domestic inflation; prices for primary products fell towards a more normal relationship with prices of imports; and finally a major part of our accumulated reserves were used in 1951/52 when a sudden fall in wool prices and a flood of imports struck us simultaneously. They have been again depleted in the last year. We have, therefore, returned to a position where we must take into account the limitations imposed on development by the costs of the associated demand for imports to a greater degree than was necessary in the immediate post-war years.

SUMMARY

It will be seen, therefore, that development is closely interwoven with the factors that affect financial stability. Briefly, the essence of this relationship can be summarised thus:

(1) Expenditure on development is a major and variable element in total expenditure, and adequate development plans, public and private, are essential to maintain full employment and to avoid the instability associated with deflation.

(2) If, however, expenditure on development tends to exceed the resources made available by savings, there will be a corresponding tendency to rising prices and other aspects of instability associated with inflation.

(3) Expenditure on development adds to the demand for imports and can in some circumstances lead to a demand which exceeds our capacity to pay for imports.

(4) Capacity to pay for imports is dependent primarily on the output of our export industries and on the terms of trade. In these the relationship of internal to overseas costs may be significant particularly if there is a substantial adverse movement in the terms of trade. A healthy relationship of internal to external costs cannot be maintained if total expenditure is excessive.

There is of course a great variety of possible situations in this complex of relationships and a glance through Australian economic history of the last generation will provide interesting case histories. But for the purposes of this paper it is probably desirable to concentrate consideration on the type of situation most relevant to our current conditions and to their probable evolution.

The dominant feature of the present Australian economy is the strength of the urge to development. This is shown not merely in the physical evidences of achievement nor in the statistics that show how formidable a proportion of our resources we devote to this purpose; it is shown also in the mood, the climate of opinion and expectation, among those who have decisions to make about development. There is a widespread conviction that Australia is in an active phase of growth and that while checks and interruptions are possible, indeed likely, they will prove temporary.

I would attribute this general sense of growth to the following features of our situation:

(1) The determination to increase our population by a steady and substantial flow of migrants—this flow, while imposing its strain on us, provides a continuing basis for expanding production and establishes a steadily expanding need for equipment of all kinds, that is it creates the need and the opportunity for development.

(2) Our primary industries are experiencing a technical revolution, which, if applied widely and supported by the necessary capital expenditure, offers the opportunity for both greatly increased output and relatively lower costs.

(3) The steady policy of industrialisation has produced the basis of an industrial community—skilled workers, technicians, managers—basic industrial services, and a wider range of supporting forms of production on which further expansion can be based.

(4) Overseas industrialists have become increasingly conscious of the possibilities of Australia both as a growing market and as the source of productive capacity.

(5) We are gradually evolving a more adequately equipped and skilled market for capital with specialised financial institutions capable of servicing the varied financial needs of the economy.

These factors are strong and apparently persistent and at least while conditions in the major industrial countries of the world remain buoyant there seems good reason to expect their continuance. While judgments of this kind are, of course, dangerous, it seems to me that we can expect this expansionist phase to continue and that, therefore, we are more likely to be concerned in the years ahead with the problem of finding the resources to give effect to the plans for development that emerge naturally from the homes, the businesses, and the governments of Australia than we are to be concerned with a deficiency of plans with which to keep our people and our resources at work.

In other words, the questions we may have to answer are:

(1) How can we increase the resources available for development? And when we have done our utmost—

(2) How can we limit our developmental plans so that we do not press against the limits of our internal and external resources to the point of financial instability?

POSSIBILITIES OF INCREASING RESOURCES FOR DEVELOPMENT

What are the possibilities of adding to our resources for development?

Increased production. Often it is suggested that if we can produce more by increasing our population and by raising our productivity per head we can add correspondingly to our rate of development. It is true that there is scope by these means to increase total production although it may be less than generally believed. The last decade has been a period of remarkable population growth and very heavy capital investment, yet it is unlikely that the average increase per year in G.N.P.

(apart from the effect of price increases) over that period has exceeded 4 per cent. This of course understates the full effect of population and productivity changes: part of the increase is taken out in increased leisure and also in changes in the nature of goods and services produced. Many of the things on which money is spent as income rises are less likely to be influenced by factors increasing production per head— some forms of entertainment, travel, clothing, and other personal possessions, services, and so on, are by their nature less subject to economies of mass production than many of the more essential items of production, but their inclusion in production may be more indicative of rising standards of living than mere increases in the value of production per head.

Only a part of the increase resulting from higher production can be applied to development. The newcomers and those whose output is increased by higher productivity will receive corresponding incomes and will spend the major part of them on consumption. Only to the extent that their incomes are saved are additional resources made available for development. Thus a 4 per cent increase in G.N.P., which is perhaps more than we can expect year in year out, can be expected to give a potential increase of only about 4 per cent in the volume of resources available for development. This at present value of production would mean an increase for all investment expenditure of about £40m. per year.

Another qualification associated with increasing population is the equipment needs of the new arrivals. The capital equipment required to service our population at present standards, taking into account housing, domestic equipment, schools, hospitals and other social equipment, and transport, power, factories, shops and offices and other production equipment represents a substantial amount per head.

Unless the economy has already equipment adequate for a population greater than the present one, it will need to devote a part of its development resources to equipping the new population at existing standards before it can carry its development to the stage of raising the amount of equipment per head. In other words, a larger population is in a sense an alternative to a better equipped population, and if we set ourselves too high a target rate of growth of population we may be forced to accept a slower rate of improvement in the standard of our equipment per head.

These qualifications do not suggest that it is not of great importance to increase our population and to raise our productivity, but merely that we should recognise the limitations on what we can hope to achieve by these means in the way of more rapid development.

Increased savings. Another hopeful line may be in the possibilities of greater savings. Here we start from a position in which Australians' performance is good. Despite our reputation for extravagance we are among the thriftiest people in the world. Our savings per head can be matched only in such countries as Canada, New Zealand, and the United States of America. To some extent this reflects our high standards of income and partly the relatively modest and stable consumption habits of our primary producers, but it reflects also the effectiveness of our institutions for collective savings—savings banks, life assurance societies, pension funds—as well as the practice of companies of ploughing back for expansion a substantial part of their profits.

The recent rapid growth in the use of hire purchase facilities has had the effect of diverting more savings to the provision of consumers' durable goods which contribute less than other forms of equipment to future standards of production. This diversion is at its greatest while the use of hire purchase facilities is growing and a continuance of the growth at the same rate as the last two years could limit significantly the resources available for development.

Can savings be increased from their already high level? Something could perhaps be done by changes in the tax structure so as to favour the saver as against the spender and the company that ploughs back its earnings as against the company that distributes. Colin Clark has made an ingenious plea for taxation of expenditure rather than of income and recent work in the United Kingdom may help overcome the frightening administrative difficulties which such a plan offers. The idea is certainly worth examination. The extension of pension schemes into industries and occupations employing workers on a weekly basis has become a widespread feature of United States industry, and if developed here could tap a field of income with great saving potential. So far our trade union leaders have shown much less interest in such plans than their American counterparts—but if the means test for old age pensioners is sufficiently modified their interest may be quickened.

Saving can in a sense be imposed on people by taxation and indeed to the extent that developmental work is financed from revenue it may be said that this is already being done. Theoretically it would be possible to extend this principle further and development would benefit, provided taxpayers responded by reducing their consumption rather than their own savings. The precise effect would be difficult to assess but the ultimate limitation is the willingness of the community to allow itself to be taxed.

There are clearly possibilities here, but we would be unwise to expect that we could so change consumption and savings habits as to add greatly to the resources for development even in the long run. Even now we may be fighting a losing battle with the wiles of the advertisers.

Increased production or greater saving could contribute to development by giving to it greater domestic resources. The need to pay for imports, increased by expenditure on development, may also impose a restraint on our plans. We must look, therefore, at what can be done to increase our capacity to pay for imports.

Overseas borrowing. One of the quickest methods of adding to our resources for development, if it is practicable, is to borrow abroad—either by public authority loans or by encouraging private investors to bring their funds to Australia. These have added substantially to our development potential in the last decade.

I have mentioned earlier that there is a growing interest in Australia as a field for investment. This has been reflected in a substantial flow of private capital and in the governmental loans from the I.B.R.D. and other overseas sources. Most of this has come with little direct persuasion and it may be that if we sought to do so we could make Australia an even more attractive field of opportunity for overseas capital.

But here there are three problems. First, there is a danger that in increasing our borrowings from overseas we will so increase the claims which non-Australians have on our production that they will become embarrassing either in relation to our total production or in relation to our export income. This is not a serious problem for Australia. The service of our foreign owned capital does not represent a major part of our international income and we could increase it without great concern—particularly if we could see the capital being used to increase the international income itself.

Secondly, there is the problem of the uncertainty in the flow of foreign capital. An economy receiving capital from overseas gradually gears the structure of its production to that flow. If it is suddenly interrupted (as it was for instance in 1929), there may be acute embarrassments and possibly the need for substantial changes in the pattern of domestic production. Arrangements of the kind that have run over the last decade between Australia and the I.B.R.D., by which a series of loans was arranged, represent a useful device to offset this danger, but it is difficult to see this technique being applied widely in the private sector, although the steady ploughing back of profits earned has the same sort of effect.

Thirdly, there is the political problem of how far we wish to extend foreign ownership of Australian assets and enterprises. Generally, our experience with non-Australian owners of enterprises in this country has given little cause for concern, but there is room for wide differences of opinion on how far it is wise to go.

Finally, of course, the possibilities in this field are limited by what overseas institutions and investors are prepared to invest in Australia.

It would be easy to expect too much from such a source.

Increase in export production. There is no doubt that expenditure on improvements, major irrigation, and other developmental works, together with the application of existing and growing technology, is expanding and can greatly expand our export production. However, a number of factors limit the rate at which this can be done:

(1) The scope for the opening up of unused lands is not great and where it exists requires slow and expensive preliminary development.

(2) The use of the new technology requires capital expenditure, new knowledge, and time.

(3) Some of the initial increase in productivity is generally (and wisely) taken out in the greater security of better rotations, safer stocking, and other aspects of better and safer farming rather than in increased output.

(4) Farm development is traditionally financed from internal sources —ploughing back of profits and bank borrowing against equity already built up. It is difficult for farmers, however good, to find finance for potential production.

There is need for thought on how these limiting factors can be minimised since our need of exports is great and day by day our growing population is eating into our export surpluses.

Import replacement. Since the extension of our basic export industries must be a slow process, it is natural that attention should be concentrated on the possibilities of directing development at the replacement of imports by local production. To the extent that this can be achieved development serves a double purpose. In a sense it provides some part of its own requirements of imports by the savings which it makes by meeting other people's needs for goods previously imported. Furthermore, by diversifying our production, it reduces our dependence on the income from a few major export industries and thus adds to the insulating value of our international reserves. There is also the additional advantage that most import-replacing production is not limited by the sorts of factors that restrain the growth of our primary industries. Sources of capital are readily available, up to the minute overseas techniques can be acquired and used, and production at full rate of flow follows promptly on capital expenditure.

There is no doubt that the concentration on import replacement that has characterised our development since the war has a rational justification and can contribute greatly to solving the international problems created by the development itself. But there are qualifications. The production locally of goods previously imported is not a net gain, since almost invariably the production itself involves imports—of materials, components, capital goods—and frequently requires payments of other sorts—capital charges, royalties, etc. The net saving in import expenditure may be small, and, indeed, it is possible in the period of expansion when capital equipment is being imported for the developing industry to make greater payments abroad than it saves. Moreover, it is possible that we could build up a pattern of import requirements of industry that would be very inflexible in the face of a serious deterioration in our terms of trade, so that restriction of imports would fall directly on the means to production and employment.

These problems may be the greater if development is unduly concentrated on production of final consumers' goods running ahead of the base on which they stand—the production of materials, fuels, power, transport, and the like. There may be some reason to believe that our own development is somewhat top-heavy in its superstructure in this way.

MEANS FOR LIMITING DEVELOPMENT EXPENDITURE

There is undoubted scope for extending the practicable rate of development by action in the fields I have run through briefly. Yet, if I am right that we can reasonably hope for a continuance of the factors stimulating our development, we must expect to find ourselves pressing against the limits set internally by the resources available after consumption demands have been met and externally by the pressure of expenditure on the international resources available for imports. We must expect therefore, that our governments and banking institutions will from time to time find it necessary to restrain development so as to preserve reasonable financial stability. Are effective measures practicable?

Expenditure on development may be undertaken by governments and other public authorities, or by private firms and individuals. In Australia developmental expenditure by public authorities is brought under review in the annual budgets and loan programs and there is some co-ordination at the Loan Council. It has been shown that this co-ordination can effectively discipline these programs—the growth of their aggregate has in recent years been reasonably held—taking into account the growth of the national production. Here there is no problem of knowledge or technique, but a problem of judgment and will.

Private expenditure on investment presents a much more difficult problem. It is diverse in character and widely distributed. Knowledge of its prospective changes is imperfect and there are no means whereby those conceiving and executing plans can become aware of the effect of the plans of others or be forced to reconcile conflicting plans.

In many countries governments seek to bring about such a reconciliation by control over investment projects or by control of capital issues. In Australia, except in war or threat of war, such measures are constitutionally impracticable. Here we have at our disposal the instruments of budgetary policy and monetary and banking policy. Budgetary policy is the basic instrument of economic policy and it can be used to exercise restraint or to provide a stimulus to expenditure. To some extent the restraint or stimulus can be directed so as to affect particular forms of expenditure such as expenditure on development, but there are limits. Fundamentally the public sees the budget as the means the government uses to finance its activities and of distributing the cost equitably among its citizens. Too great a variation in the content of the budget for reasons of economic policy impairs the plain man's basis of judgment of its reasonableness and its equity. Above all the budget cannot be violently altered frequently. Nevertheless, Australian history has shown the value of a soundly conceived budget policy and the dangers of irresponsibility towards basic economic problems in its formulation.

Monetary and banking policy too have their part to play and something is undoubtedly achieved by them. However, our less fully developed money market, our conviction that interest rates should be kept low, render our techniques less complete and the influence of monetary and banking policy probably less effective in the restraint of a tendency to overspending than in some other countries.

These are issues which will no doubt be explored further by others. I must, however, confess that I feel that there is some danger to the Australian economy if we cannot evolve ways of exercising effective restraint on our healthy but exuberant tendency to want to do more than our resources will permit.

CONCLUSIONS

Finally, I shall bring together the broad conclusions which I feel emerge from this survey.

(1) There seems good reason to believe that the conditions underlying Australia's recent rapid development are soundly based and that the urge to expansion will continue.

(2) That there are, however, real limits, both internal and external, to the rate of development Australia should undertake if it is to maintain financial stability.

(3) That when all possible has been done to push back these limits, we will be able to achieve much but probably less than most of us would like.

(4) We are likely therefore to be faced from time to time with

the need to restrain developmental plans, both public and private. (5) There are significant weaknesses, partly constitutional, partly technical, but partly arising from our own attitudes, in our capacity to restrain excessive expenditure on development especially when the initiative lies predominantly in the private sector of the economy.

A Matter of Prices

MUST prices always rise? The problem has, I believe, been posed sharply by what has been happening over the last two or three years. We had, at the end of the war, the normal aftermath of inflation when the excess demand built up by wartime abstention from spending and the accumulation of the means of payment produced an inflation of quite classic textbook character. This was demand inflation and its nature was well understood. Its effects have by now been substantially worked out, and it seems certain that what has been happening in more recent years is of a different character. Despite the fact that the excess demand of the post-war inflationary period has been substantially worked out, prices have continued to rise although the rate of increase has been slower than previously. The characteristic pattern seems now to be a tendency for prices to rise more or less steadily by about 3 per cent a year. Moreover, a significant new factor appears to have entered into the situation—that is a widespread acceptance of price increases of this order as natural and inevitable.

An important reason for believing that this trend of prices does in fact represent a significant and continuing element in our economic climate is the experience of the United States during the recent business recession when, despite the fact that almost every indicator of economic activity turned downwards, consumer prices continued to rise. Between August 1957 and April 1958 the index of industrial production fell by 13 per cent, retail sales by 5 per cent, and unemployment almost doubled, but the consumer price index and wage rates rose—by almost 3 per cent. The situation in Australia, though not as pronounced, is not unlike that in the United States. June figures reveal that the interim retail price index is 2·6 per cent higher than it was a year ago in spite of uncertainties in general economic conditions, which suggests that the economy needed some stimulus if growing unemployment was to be

Presidential Address, Thirty-fourth Congress, ANZAAS, Perth, August 1959. Reproduced by permission of *Economic Record* and the *Australian Journal of Science*.

avoided. In the past, periods of declining economic activity have almost invariably brought falling prices—even though the decline of retail prices has been much less than that of materials and basic foodstuffs. If this change in the relationship of price movements to other indicators is due to continuing factors, it would bring about a vital change in people's attitudes towards prices—a change which could have profound economic effects. Previously, even if people felt that the long-term trend would be upwards, they had to take into account that there would be times when prices would fall. This probability introduced some uncertainty into any assessment they were making. In other words, while the long-term trend of prices might be upwards, any judgment relating to a particular period had always to allow for the possibility of a fall. This prevented people from being able to plan on the assumption of continuously rising prices. Recent experience suggests that this may be no longer true.

If recent events here and abroad can be interpreted in this way and we can expect prices to rise always and even in times of slight economic recession by 2–3 per cent per year, and the risks of occasional reversals in this trend are remote, we face, I believe, a very serious economic problem. Of course, it is not a problem of the same human urgency as the unemployment and stagnation of the 1930s and there are, I know, people who would dispute that it is a problem at all. I am satisfied, however, that this attitude is based on a failure to realise the consequences of the continuance of this trend. I propose in this address therefore

(1) to examine the question of whether this slow deterioration in the value of money, this creeping inflation, matters to the economy and to the people who compose it;

(2) to examine briefly the attitudes which underlie the decisions which produce rising prices and to pose certain questions to test whether these attitudes are valid for the groups of people who hold them;

(3) to consider the practicability of a stable price level and the conditions which would be necessary to achieve it;

(4) to throw out certain ideas about institutional and political changes which might promote these conditions.

I do not expect to produce final answers on these matters—but I believe that if economists, administrators, political groups, and the public generally can turn their minds to this problem as they did to the problem of unemployment in the 1930s, there will emerge the insight necessary to its solution.

CREEPING INFLATION: DOES IT MATTER?

Some people argue that, since we have accepted full employment as an objective of policy—an objective which we can achieve— it is inevitable that prices will move upwards and we might just as well make the best of it. They point out that there are ways for people to protect themselves against the consequences and that there is evidence that many people are already trying to do so. They are attempting to protect their incomes by means of automatic adjustments and other escalator clauses in contracts and their wealth by diversifying their assets to include real property and equities which offer a hedge against inflation. It is sometimes suggested that the current boom in the prices of shares and other equities on the world's stock exchanges reflects a growing conviction that rising prices must be expected and a growing determination to insure against their effects.

Another view is that creeping inflation is not only inevitable but desirable—that slowly rising prices stimulate investment and reduce the burden of indebtedness on the active section of the community. They give windfall profits to industry and fill capitalists with confident hopes for the future. Thus, it is argued, they give an impetus to development and are consequently generally in the social interest.

These views have a specious charm, but I believe they require critical examination. The presumption that it is possible to take reasonably effective action against the effects of rising prices is based upon the experience of a very small financially conscious minority operating in a community, the great majority of which is in the grip of what Keynes called 'the money illusion'—the belief that the value of a unit of money is constant. The longer prices continue to rise—however slowly—and the more confident become the expectations of further rises, the more people will seek protection and the more expensive it will become. Indeed, it is difficult to conceive an upward trend of prices remaining slow and gradual in a world where everybody is seeking to protect him- self against its effects. Thus the very possibility of inflation remaining at a creeping rate, as well as the possibility of the wise guy being able to hedge his risks, may depend on there being sufficient uncertainty about the continuance of the trend to preserve the money illusion in the majority of the people.

I believe it is true that slowly rising prices have a stimulating effect on business enterprise and thereby tend to promote industrial and commercial development. It does this, of course, by increasing the share of the national income which goes to profit earners at the expense of the rest of the community. It is a form of subsidy—but a subsidy which is not voted by parliament or subject to any critical examination by the Tariff Board or any other judicial authority. It has been fairly described by Knut Wicksell, the great Swedish economist, as capitalist confiscation. I believe that a high rate of development is an essential element in economic policy, and if it is necessary for the community to subsidise it I see no objection to this being done—but let it be done in a way in which the community can see for what purposes and for whose benefit it is taxing itself and in a way which enables the burden to be distributed with some degree of social justice.

It should be noted also that the effect of rising prices in inflating profit incomes is not confined to the investment field. Some of the windfall is certainly devoted to increasing consumption expenditure—diverting resources into those classes of goods of particular interest to profit earners. This is one of a number of distortions in the use of resources which flows from creeping inflation. Another is in the investment field itself. The advantages derived by industrial and commercial development are partly at the expense of public and social development. There is, I believe, good reason to feel that the provision of transport, water supply, and power tends to lag behind the growth of industry and commerce and that schools, universities, hospitals, and other social equipment suffer by comparison, as does also housing. We may well have reached a stage in the development of our standards of living when the greatest improvement can be obtained from the improvement in the physical environment in which we live and in the development of services co-operatively provided rather than in the further accumulation of personal possessions. The city of Perth is giving a fine example of the way in which the quality of life can be enhanced for all by intelligent collective use of resources in the physical environment and the social institutions which compose it. A gracious city—well equipped with well-planned roads and highways, with parks and playing fields, providing fine schools, universities, public buildings, theatres, and the like—may well give a better life for its citizens than one which lacks these amenities but sprouts television antennae from every roof top and whose streets are jammed with opulent chromium studded motor vehicles.

Another distortion which can be produced by creeping inflation arises from the conflict of objectives which it can create for the monetary authorities. The Commonwealth Bank, for example, is required by law to pursue a policy which will best contribute to the maintenance of full employment and to the stability of the currency. These are the basic objectives of monetary policy in practically all democratic countries. If there is a tendency for prices to rise, the monetary authority may feel obliged to impose a restrictive credit policy even though such a policy may prevent the emergence of full employment. In the United States at the present time it seems clear that credit policy is restrictive and interest rates are at their highest level for many years, despite the existence of a substantial body of unemployed. This policy is due, I believe, to the fear of inflation.

Finally, the view that rising prices do not matter tends to ignore the international aspects of our economy. We are major international traders, and our capacity to carry through a rapid development program depends upon our exports commanding prices which give a significant margin over costs of production and upon our domestic costs being at a level which makes the establishment and growth of import replacing industries attractive to domestic and overseas capital. It is true that for some years after the war our exports commanded excellent prices and enabled us to buy imports of finished goods, materials, and capital equipment on very favourable terms. In such circumstances it can be and was reasonably argued that rising domestic prices were desirable to pass on to other sections of the community a share in the remarkable prosperity of our basic industries. That time has gone, at least for the present. Import prices have continued to rise and export prices have come back, following periodic breaks in the market, to a degree which made our terms of trade in 1958/59 not much better than in the depression years of the 1930s. For the future we must rely increasingly on our capacity to reduce real costs of production by increasing productivity through better technology and our ability to keep the movement of our internal money costs favourable compared with those in competitive countries.

For these reasons, I suggest we should receive, with grave scepticism, pronouncements which suggest that we do not need to worry about prices. A persistent tendency for prices to rise may, like the housemaid's baby, be very small at first—but once people have got used to it being around, they may well be astonished at how rapidly it will grow.

CREEPING INFLATION: BASIC ATTITUDES

The tendency of prices to creep upwards in periods when total demand is not excessive and even when it is mildly deficient derives in part from the attitudes of people—those who make decisions in business and those whose passivity towards such decisions reduces the natural resistance to higher prices. Let us look for a moment at some of these attitudes and consider how far they are wisely based and in the interests of those who hold them.

Take first the pricing policies of industrialists and traders. No doubt some degree of competition prevails over a wide range of industry and commerce, but there are degrees of monopoly and tacitly accepted practices which mean that prices are determined by management rather than by the market for a wide range of goods and that within significant margins producers can decide at what prices their goods shall be sold.

In these circumstances the policies of the management are important.

Firstly, management appears to assume that increases in costs should and can be passd on—and, so far as can be judged from the evidence available, it appears to be broadly true that in Australia such increases in manufacturing and distributive industry can, in fact, be passed on. Whether this is due to a high degree of monopoly in our industrial structure, elements which are being increased by the current popularity of 'take-overs', or to inadequately developed price-consciousness on the part of our consumers is difficult to judge. But it tends to make our industries less responsive than they should be to measures which by increasing productivity could reduce costs or alternatively avoid their being increased.

A similar attitude seems to prevail towards the results of improvements in productivity. In manufacturing industry, especially, there is a strong trend towards methods which reduce the unit cost of production —sometimes in quite dramatic terms. It is hard, however, to find examples of products which as a consequence are sold to the consumer at lower prices. Manufacturers in such circumstances will sometimes produce a better article at the old price—they will frequently produce a more elaborate article or one which is more expensively advertised or sold with more elaborate and prestige building services. The trend over recent years for the costs of advertising, packaging, and retailing to absorb an increasing proportion of the final selling price to the consumer is a clear indication of the industrialist's conviction that to reduce prices is not good business.

This attitude makes it difficult, if not impossible, for the community at large to obtain the benefits of increasing productivity through being able to buy at lower prices and therefore having a surplus to devote to other forms of consumption or to savings. It is true that improvements in the quality of goods can provide real improvement in the standard of living. But there is a point beyond which further improvement in technical quality has little significance for the need the commodity is designed to meet. When this level is reached, only vanity and social status are served by further increases in standard of quality. Unwillingness to pass on the benefits of increased productivity in lower prices has great significance for wages, to which I wish to turn in a few moments.

Another important element in the pricing policy of industrialists and traders is their belief that selling prices should be sufficient to provide not merely cover for costs of production, including a reasonable return on capital, but also a substantial part of the additional capital required for expansion. Undistributed profits after the payment of dividends at normal rates provide a very substantial part of the development funds

of Australian companies. In recent years this tendency in pricing policy
has been extended to include major public instrumentalities, with consequential increases in prices of services to consumers.

While we are faced with a shortage of capital it is difficult to blame
companies for ensuring the funds for growth in this way—indeed, so
important and stable an element are undistributed profits in our total
supply of savings that I personally would wish to see them encouraged.
But it is important to note that they pre-empt a considerable part of
available savings to particular enterprises and so intensify the monopolistic elements in our economic organisation and make it more difficult
for smaller and newer enterprises to be financed. Also prices designed to
provide such surpluses include a kind of unofficial indirect tax imposed
on consumers for the benefit of the industrialists and traders concerned.
It is interesting to speculate on possible ways of giving the community
generally some of the benefit of the equity built up by this tax while
continuing to encourage the savings themselves.

It is possible for prices to be managed in this way partly because of
the widespread semi-monopolistic elements in contemporary productive
and distributive organisation and partly because general demand has
been maintained for a number of years at high levels and appears likely
to be so maintained. This is a new feature in the situation. In the past,
even those industrialists with substantially monopolistic positions have
thought it wise to stimulate demand in times of declining economic
activity by reducing prices. Such declines now come more rarely and are
less severe. Furthermore, governments and central banks have shown
that they can be relied upon to take reasonably prompt action to counter
any serious threat to total demand. If this can confidently be relied upon
industrialists may well conclude that it will pay them to 'ride out' periods
of falling demand without reducing their prices. In the absence of some
uncertainty about the future of demand, the weapon of price reductions
may fall into rusty disuse.

Monetary theorists may argue that the capacity of business to
administer prices in the way I have described depends upon the money
supply increasing or the rate of turnover of money rising sufficiently
and that consequently the instruments of control lie in our own hands. I
think this is formally correct. However, our experience suggests the
money supply and the velocity of circulation are capable of some automatic adjustment. A sense of increased need on the part of business
enterprises for a larger money supply will tend to produce the desired
increase and even to the extent that it does not there is a variety of
means by which the existing money supply can be made to turn over
more rapidly.

In a system which operates on overdraft accounts in which there is at any time a substantial margin of undrawn limits, the possibility of increased advances adding to the volume of deposits is clear. Apart from customers with recorded limits there are others whose relationships with their bankers are such that they could without difficulty increase their indebtedness beyond that provided for in existing formal under-standings. Bank advances can therefore be expected to respond to some extent automatically to increased demands on them.

Similarly, in circumstances of rising needs for working capital reflect-ing a gradual upward movement in the price and income structure, it is not unlikely that the flow of credit funds through the capital market to industry and commerce would be speeded up without significant increase in the money supply itself. In addition, we have seen in recent years institutional developments which have increased the rate of turn-over of the money supply. Outstanding illustrations would be the development of hire purchase companies financed largely by short-term borrowing and the emergence of firms specialising in the short-term money market.

These elements of flexibility in the money supply and the tendency for it to respond to some extent automatically to the demands which the money-using community makes on it mean that the outline I have given of the influence of management decisions in the formation of prices is not inconsistent with monetary theory.

It is true that a monetary policy directed to preventing any upward movement in prices generally could be made effective if it were suffi-ciently restrictive to offset the automatic response of the money supply to increased demands on it. But this could be difficult to achieve and might have other consequences such as declining employment which would make it impracticable or unwise.

Let us turn now to the critical issue of wage rates, which is in many respects the core of this problem. We must start with a recognition of the fact that we are in a world of rising productivity—where the con-tinuing accumulation of capital and the growth of science and tech-nology are increasing the output of agriculture and industry per unit of labour employed. This much advertised quality of our economic organisation is known, of course, to wage earners, and they, not unnaturally, and in my personal judgment very properly, expect that they will obtain a reasonable share of the higher standards of consump-tions which this increasing productivity should make possible.

This expectation is very generally held to be reasonable, and that the Commonwealth Arbitration Commission itself is guided by it is, I believe, a reasonable inference from its recent judgments. For instance, in its judgment on the 1958 basic wage inquiry, the Commission stated that the worker was entitled to his share of this increased productivity and the basic wage should from time to time make provision for it.

These attitudes, however reasonable, can, when taken in association with the attitudes of industrialists and traders towards prices within their management, have explosive effects. Consider the following chain of propositions which, while they are over-simplified, do, I believe, outline a set of relationships which are significantly influencing the pattern of our economy.

(1) Because productivity is rising, wage earners believe they are entitled to higher real wages and, to the extent that they cannot be convinced that they are receiving them as a result of falling prices, will seek higher money wages.

(2) Unless the Arbitration Commission can be convinced that wage earners' living standards are rising to a degree consistent with output per head, they will approve increased wage rates.

(3) Since industrialists and traders are reluctant to allow rising productivity to be reflected in lower prices, wage earners cannot obtain higher real wages without wage increases.

(4) Accordingly, rising money wage rates are inevitable, but since industrialists and traders generally are able to pass on such increases in higher prices and make a practice of doing so, the benefit from money wage increases to the wage earner may well prove illusory.

You may feel sceptical of propositions which appear to suggest that wage earners have gained little or nothing from increased wage rates over recent decades. But it is not suggested that wage earners' standards of living have not improved—indeed the improvement is obvious. But I do suggest that when allowance is made for higher aggregate earnings due to freedom from unemployment, larger family incomes as a result of more overtime, more readily available casual work, higher relative earnings for young people, for the effects of increased social services, and for the benefits of durable consumers' goods financed by savings stimulated by hire purchase facilities, there will be surprisingly little left to be attributed to higher real wage rates.

I suggest to trade unions and to other representatives of wage earners that it may be worth their while to consider whether their efforts to improve the living standards of their members might not be better directed along different channels—whether, provided full employment is maintained, their interests would not be better served by higher real wages made possible by falling prices—whether better, and cheaper, and more social services like the educational and medical benefits now provided would not improve their standard more and free some of their current income for other more personal purposes—whether even in respect of higher money incomes it would not be better to seek these from the redistributive effects of the taxation and expenditure powers of the government rather than primarily through higher money wages where the benefits can apparently so easily be taken from them.

The attitudes of industrialists and traders would also bear examination from a rational long-term view of their own interests. Their anxiety to pass on cost increases and their distaste for lower prices as a reflection of increasing productivity are attitudes which have evolved during a phase of our development when Australian industry has been heavily protected by tariffs and by distance. It reflects, too, the influence of American business thought which has evolved in a large, wealthy and largely self-contained market with a very high rate of productivity growth. In Australian conditions, given our community's attitude towards wages, each industry's prices contribute to and in the aggregate form a large proportion of the costs of production of other industries. Especially in an era where the surplus provided by an unusually competitive and dominant export industry appears to be being progressively narrowed, there may be room for a conventional understanding among industrialists and traders that they will abstain from increasing one another's costs and will, as opportunity offers, reduce them, to their mutual advantage, by reducing their selling prices.

I was interested to read this week that Mr Blough, the Chairman of U.S. Steel, is opposing a rise in the wage rates of steel workers on the grounds that it would be inflationary. Even if the steel industry could absorb the increase without raising prices, he argues, it would tend to raise other wage rates where the cost could not be absorbed. He fears that the United States will drift slowly into the oblivion of the Greeks and the Romans unless it can disabuse itself of the idea that working men are entitled to a wage increase each and every year. I feel that Mr Blough would have more hope of persuading the steel workers that they should be concerned about the fate which awaits the United States if the practice of his company and his fellow industrialists had been to pass on to the public in lower prices the benefits of increasing productivity which he admits is taking place. Unless he finds an alternative way of satisfying his workers' legitimate expectations, the inflation he fears may well become a reality.

Above all, there seems to be room for a revision of our attitudes as consumers. I have always been puzzled at the passivity of the Australian public towards rising prices. Perhaps it is because our money is spent by women but our opinions and our protests—in public at least—are expressed by men. Certainly for the sovereign authority of the economic textbook we are surprisingly pusillanimous and distressingly willing to allow our tastes and desires to be dictated by those whose primary motive is to take money from us. There is room for a more critical consumer's attitude towards prices and a greater scepticism to the incitements of the advertiser and the salesman. There is room for more investigation and research for the protection and guidance of the buying public and for the exploration of ways of adding to the scope and quality of individuals' lives and of the forms of production and expenditure which would best contribute to them.

I believe the changes of attitudes I have advocated are possible— indeed, that they can well be justified by the intelligent self-interest of the parties concerned. But they are, of course, more likely to occur and to be effective in a community which has demonstrated its desire and its capacity to combine stable purchasing power in its money with full employment and progressive development.

CONDITIONS FAVOURING PRICE STABILITY

There are, in my opinion, certain essentials if price stability is to be achieved without sacrifice of full employment and development. The more rapidly productivity is growing, the more readily widely held expectations of rising living standards can be met and the more margin there will be for the absorption of higher money costs without increasing prices. But the rate of productivity growth can be influenced by our own policy decisions. Firstly, there must be a high level of expenditure on research—basic and applied—and on education. These are the sources of the growth of knowledge and of skills from which increasing productivity derive. They also form a contribution to the quality of life itself. Secondly, we must, as a nation and in our businesses, be willing to spend heavily on capital equipment. It is this equipment which makes possible the application of new knowledge and technology and so produces the increasing productivity upon which rising living standards depend. But we must be willing to provide the resources for this capital expenditure by saving an adequate proportion of current income. Resources cannot be used both for capital development and for current consumption, and if they are to be available for capital purposes, then we must individually and collectively abstain from spending on consumption a sufficient proportion of our income to ensure that resources are free to be taken up for development. The present level of saving almost certainly falls short of what is required to carry through capital development at the rate which the community desires without continuing danger of inflationary pressure. I believe that it is dangerous to leave the adequacy of saving to finance development to chance or the uncertain influence of interest rates as we do at present. In this connection I have two positive suggestions to make which I believe would be worth examination. The first is that there should be general contributory superannuation supplementing the basic pensions at present provided. There seems good reason to believe that the great majority of people would be willing to contribute to such a scheme for the benefits it would confer to security in old age. But from an economic point of view, it would, with the rising population which Australia can expect over the coming decades, produce net savings of very considerable magnitude and so do much to make possible the speeding up of our national development.

A second possibility of a much more radical character is that the government should accept responsibility for determining the proportion of our gross national product which should be devoted to development, public and private, and so modify its tax system to ensure adequate savings to provide the necessary resources. To this end it would need to allow savings to be regarded as a direct alternative to the payment of taxes except to the extent that they were required to finance the government's current expenditure. The degree to which it has become necessary to impose taxation to support adequate development expenditure is perhaps not widely realised. In 1958/59 public authority expenditure on works totalled £520m. but the net increase in public indebtedness in that year was no more than £126m.

Consideration might be given to taking out from the Budget proper provision for capital expenditure and financing it from the proceeds of a development tax. As I envisage it, such a tax would nominally be designed to provide the funds to finance all forms of investment, public and private, and would

(1) fall on income at appropriately graded rates to produce whatever proportion of total incomes was judged necessary;

(2) be subject to rebate of tax, either wholly or in part for net savings voluntarily made—net savings for this purpose being defined as net worth in the usual accounting sense, but excluding unrealised capital gains or losses.

The greater the volume of voluntary saving, the smaller would be the yield of the tax. Ideally, assuming that complete rebates were granted, the yield would be nil if citizens provided adequate savings by their own choice in forms acceptable to them. Such a tax would be capable of many variations—it is in itself a variation of the Expenditure Tax proposed by Nicholas Kaldor but designed for somewhat different purposes. Like the Expenditure Tax, it would almost certainly present great administrative difficulties and might on examination prove impracticable. On the other hand, there are attractions about a form of taxation which offers certainty of adequate finance for development, public and private, which bears less heavily on those willing to save and which leaves the taxpayer with freedom to avoid the tax completely by saving voluntarily in ways which suit his own convenience.

Given a growing body of knowledge and technology and a high rate of capital investment, the means to a steadily rising standard of living should be at hand. In the interests of reasonably stable purchasing power of money it would be preferable if means could be found to raise living standards other than by the increase in wage rates. As I have said earlier, I believe that much can be done through the extension and development of free and subsidised services, of which education and medical services are illustrations, as well as by the improvement of the physical environment—our homes, our towns and cities. I personally would like to see a great extension of aid given to non-profit making bodies concerned with providing greater opportunities for the enjoyment of and participation in sporting activities and artistic and cultural pursuits. These, with greater leisure time, can greatly enrich our lives. Within the industrial field itself there is a great variety of profit sharing devices which I think merit the interest of employees and their representatives. Even in the field of money rewards I do not think we have exhausted the possibilities of the redistributive powers of government taxation and expenditure. A variation in tax scales which reduces the taxes falling on wage earners and their families or increases in money payments such as child endowment would be at least as valuable as and almost certainly more secure than an equivalent increase in wage rates.

While the institutional and political changes I have described would help create conditions in which price stability would be easier to achieve, basically we must look to the changes in attitudes of industrialists and traders, of wage earners, and of consumers, which I have urged in an earlier part of this paper. Fundamentally, prices rise because too many people wish them to rise and too few are anxious to resist. As an encouragement to your own change of heart in this matter, could I conclude by summarising the conclusions my argument leads to?

(1) It does matter if prices continue to rise—the trend is a serious and growing threat to the health of our economy; if it continues uninterrupted there is a grave danger that it will gather momentum from the efforts of people to protect themselves from its effects and cease to be merely a 'creeping inflation'.

(2) The tendency of prices to rise, even in times of mild recession, derives basically from attitudes of industrialists and traders, of wage earners and of consumers, which seem of doubtful validity even from the point of view of their own interests.

(3) Reasonable stability in the value of money can be achieved if we think it worth while—although it would be facilitated by some institutional changes designed to ensure a high rate of development backed by ample savings, and greater concentration on improvements in the standard of living by means other than money wage increases.

The Problems of
External Balance

T HE first question I want to discuss briefly is why we trade overseas. A bird's eye view (or a space-ship view) of Australia would
show that we are all busy producing a vast and motley collection
of goods and services. Some 85–90 per cent of these goods and services
are consumed within Australia. The other 10–15 per cent are swapped
for the products of other countries.

Not only in the last twelve months but throughout our history we
have suffered, from time to time, a lot of discomfort and sometimes
considerable hardship so we can go on trading in this way. A fair
question then is whether it is really worth it.

The economics textbooks defend foreign trade on the grounds that
countries, like regions within countries, are better at producing some
things than others. If this is so, it can be easily shown that we can all
benefit by concentrating on the things we can do best and exchanging
some of these products for the goods and materials which other countries
can produce most efficiently.

We can divide imports into three broad categories. First there are
the goods and materials which we cannot produce in Australia at all,
even at high cost. Some raw materials are in this category, and so far
oil is too. If we could not import them we would have to go without
and would not be able to support our present industrial structure or our
present population, let alone a growing one.

Secondly, there are the goods which we can produce in Australia but
at relatively high cost, which is the case the textbooks usually have in
mind. By importing these goods we can enjoy a higher real income than
if we produced them ourselves. We can buy more television tubes with
a bale of wool than we could make with the resources which it takes to
produce the wool. Or if we do not want more television tubes we can
buy as many as we could have made ourselves and still have some
funds or resources left over for something else.

Address to the Australian Administrative Staff College, 4 June 1961.

Finally, there are the goods which we can produce in Australia at reasonable cost, but which we still import. The benefit here comes from the wider variety and choice which foreign trade makes possible. If we look at world trade we see that it is becoming increasingly a matter of swapping manufactures for manufactures, often of rather similar goods. Motor cars are an obvious example—many countries, including Australia, are both exporters and importers. As we become richer, both as countries and as individuals, the widening of consumer choice can form an increasingly important part of rising living standards.

We might note here that foreign travel can be looked on in the same way as visible imports. Foreign travel is something which we cannot produce locally and forms an increasingly important part of many people's current or prospective standard of living.

MECHANISM OF FOREIGN TRADE

Let us turn now briefly to the mechanism of foreign trade. The most important feature, perhaps, is that the figures of imports and exports which we watch so carefully from month to month are the outcome of a vast number of decisions made by individuals and businesses. Farmers decide how much wheat they will sow and whether they will sell all their wool now or keep some back in the hope of better prices later; housewives decide whether they will buy imported sheets or saucepans or tinned fish or the local product; manufacturers decide whether they will try to find export markets or sell all their products locally, or whether they will buy an imported machine or a local one; and so on.

The other items in our balance of payments are also the outcome of many individual decisions. Mrs Smith has to decide whether she will take that overseas trip and whether she should contribute to that new world charity; Mr Jones decides whether he will send some money to his old parents in Birmingham; the X.Y.Z. Co. decides whether it will build a new factory in Australia, or how much of last year's profits it will remit to London. It would be interesting to try to add up the decisions which determine one year's balance of payments; it is hard to think of any decision regarding expenditure (from the toddler's choice of sweets up) or any decision regarding production which does not affect the balance of payments in some way.

FORCES MAKING FOR EQUILIBRIUM

As the items in our balance of payments—our receipts and payments of foreign exchange—are the outcome of so many apparently unrelated decisions, how do they ever balance?

The first explanation we can give is the bookkeeping one—the balance of payments balances because we draw it up that way. But a more helpful explanation is that it balances because any difference between receipts and payments of foreign exchange is reflected in a corresponding movement in our bank balance—i.e. our international reserves.

But when we look at reserves we find that they are not particularly large in relation to our overseas transactions. Our total overseas payments for imports, freight, travel, interest, and dividends and so on are running at around £1,500m. a year. Our reserves are around £500m. or, say, four months' payments. Are there any equilibrating forces which prevent reserves from being exhausted in times of adversity or built up to embarrassingly high levels in times of unusual prosperity?

Part of the answer is that exports and imports are not unrelated. Imports depend partly on the levels of incomes and liquidity in Australia; these levels are determined at least in part by export income. When export incomes rise the farmers become more prosperous and the community more liquid; this is usually reflected in a rise in imports, perhaps in the next year. Conversely, a fall in export incomes means a direct loss of incomes and of liquidity and usually has a dampening effect on business confidence; all these factors encourage a cutting back of import orders and a subsequent fall in actual imports.

But clearly we are not prepared to allow fluctuations in our export prices to have their full effect on domestic activity and so on imports. Balancing our international accounts is not our only or indeed our main objective; we also want to maintain high levels of employment, a high rate of economic growth, and reasonably stable prices. If export prices fall, what has really happened? Foreigners have decided to pay us less for the 10–15 per cent of our total production which we export. While this is regrettable it does not seem sufficient reason for cutting back the other 85–90 per cent of our activity if we can possibly avoid it. Conversely, if foreigners decide to pay us more for our exports, we do not want this to lead to a wild boom affecting the whole economy.

We therefore interfere with the automatic mechanism. When export income and international reserves fall we offset the fall in liquidity; one approach to this is by releasing funds from the trading banks' Statutory Reserve Deposit Accounts. Conversely, when international reserves are rising we seek to mop up some of the increase by raising the Statutory Reserve Deposit ratios or by other means. This all makes the task of balancing our receipts and payments of foreign exchange, and so avoiding wide swings in our international reserves more difficult but we believe it better serves the ends which the vast majority of Australians prefer.

POLICY MEASURES TO BRING ABOUT EQUILIBRIUM

By what means, then, can we bring about external balance? Before considering this question we should perhaps define what we mean by external balance. We do not mean that our receipts and payments of foreign exchange must be equal each year; we mean that over a period of years they should be approximately in balance. Mild swings from surplus to deficit in the balance of payments from year to year must be expected in an economy such as Australia's, but major changes will also occur from time to time depending on the state of overseas markets, seasonal conditions in Australia, the level of economic activity in Australia and international economic conditions. The purpose of holding international reserves is to act as a buffer against these fluctuations: in good years reserves will rise and in less favourable years reserves will run down.

If our external accounts are in long-term balance and international reserves are adequate to meet any short-term drains upon them, due perhaps to a temporary but sharp reduction in overseas demand for our exports, then we have no worries. If, however, our external accounts are not in a position of long-term balance or our reserves are not adequate to meet these short-term drains then we will need to consider what action is necessary to balance the position. It can be seen, however, that there are two facets to the problem—the short-term and the long-term—and different policies may be required for each.

In most developing countries, such as Australia, the problem has been mainly one of avoiding deficits in the balance of payments and we might take a look at the main policy measures available to deal with this situation.

Monetary policy, through the influence it can exert on the level of internal demand, can be used to reduce the rate of flow of imports with a consequent improvement in the balance of payments position. However, we have already seen that balancing our international accounts is not our only objective and therefore care has to be taken to ensure that the level of overall demand is not pushed down to a point where it is insufficient to keep the economy, its workers and its equipment reasonably fully employed. This conflict of objectives is extremely difficult to resolve by the use of monetary policy alone.

Import restrictions have been used by many countries as the main means of ensuring external balance. As you all know, Australia has had restrictions on imports since just before the last world war and it was only in February 1960 that we became virtually free of import controls. Although they are a fairly certain method of keeping imports within the bounds of our foreign exchange income, they cannot be regarded as an appropriate way of correcting a long-term deficit in the balance of payments. Their main disadvantage is that they do nothing to improve the underlying imbalance, but in fact allow the imbalance to widen. Behind the cloak of import restrictions, costs and prices tend to get further out of line with costs in other countries. The lack of competition from imported goods results in rises in the price of home produced goods; whilst the incidental protection afforded to inefficient industries raises costs. In addition, import controls divert capital resources into forms of production that are uneconomic and give no encouragement to the production of goods for export.

Devaluation of the currency is another measure which has been advocated as an answer to the problems of a country with a long-term balance of payments deficit. Devaluation of a country's currency relative to all other currencies raises the prices of all its imports and, depending upon whether prices for its exports are determined locally or on overseas markets, either makes its exports cheaper to the foreign buyer or increases the profitability of exporting. In either case an expansion of exports could be expected. It is argued that this would tend to bring about a better balance in the country's overseas trade and a consequent improvement in the overall balance of payments position. On the other hand the expected improvement depends very largely upon the response of overseas buyers and local exporters to the changes in prices and incomes which the devaluation brings about. Consequently there is no guarantee that even a substantial devaluation would achieve an improvement in the balance of trade sufficient to balance the overall position. In addition it is likely that the higher incomes generated in the devaluing country would be reflected in a rise in domestic prices and costs which could nullify to a large extent the advantages derived from the devaluation. The effects of devaluation on the inflow of capital are also uncertain, but they could be serious.

Other measures which could be taken in an endeavour to overcome a continuing deficit include the more widespread use of tariffs on imports, subsidies on exports, and perhaps higher taxes on goods with a high import content or on goods which could be exported. As with a devaluation, the object of these measures is primarily to make imports dearer and exporting more profitable. However, they would also tend to raise the level of domestic prices and costs and would be extremely difficult to administer. There is also the danger that once imposed, taxes and, more particularly, tariffs would prove difficult to remove.

I have briefly touched upon these measures in order to underline the uncertainties which exist when economic policy making is under consideration. I think you will agree that it is very difficult to make a confident decision as to which measure would be most likely to achieve the desired result. In fact, a combination of the measures may be most appropriate.

OUR PRESENT PROBLEMS

This brings us to our present balance of payments problems.

Let us go back to early 1960. The situation then seemed fairly satisfactory:

(1) Reserves were over £500m. and we also had drawing rights on the International Monetary Fund.

(2) Export prices had recovered nicely from the 1958/59 low; the export price index in January 1960 was 21 per cent higher than a year earlier.

(3) Export volume was increasing steadily; the wool clip had risen by 10 per cent in 1958/59 and was expected to be up another 6 per cent in 1959/60.

(4) Imports had been held at around £800m. for several years, and although administrative difficulties might have increased there was little evidence that the demand for imported goods was pressing strongly against the restrictions, at least before inflation got well under way in 1959/60.

The government therefore decided in February, as part of its anti-inflationary program, to remove nearly all remaining import restrictions. It was thought that increased import competition would have a generally beneficial effect in helping to restore internal balance between supply and demand and in helping to reduce prices. Also, of course, this move was consistent with the broad policy of returning as soon as possible to the system of allowing import decisions to be made in the market-place rather than administratively.

Unfortunately, the fates were already conspiring against us. In the very month in which restrictions were removed export prices fell by 4 per cent and then went on falling until by January 1961 the index for wool was 14 per cent lower than a year earlier and the overall index 13 per cent lower. If export prices had been the same on average in the financial year just ending as in 1950/60 export income would have been significantly higher, and our whole balance of payments position would be rather different.

The volume of wool production was also 5 per cent lower in 1960/61. While increases of the 1958/59-1959/60 order could not be expected to continue indefinitely, this particular fall came at an unfortunate time.

Thirdly, it seems that unsatisfied or latent demands for imported goods were stronger than was realised, or that stocks had run down further, or that the time lags are greater. Whatever the reason, imports increased sharply around mid-1960 and showed no signs of falling until March 1961.

The main item in the balance of payments that turned out much better than expected is capital inflow, and this has helped to sustain reserves. Some of this capital inflow, however, seems to be due to delayed payment for imports and could be quickly reversed.

MAKING THE DECISIONS

Before we talk about our balance of payments prospects let us turn to the question of decision making. We have seen that the government and Reserve Bank were faced in 1960 by these problems:

(1) At home there was strong inflationary pressure.

(2) Imports were still subject to restrictions, but there seemed a good chance that if inflationary pressures could be eliminated imports would not exceed our capacity to pay for them at then current export prices.

(3) The longer-term balance of payments prospects were uncertain, but it seemed likely that in any case we would have to strengthen export income.

The decisions which were taken in February 1960 and since then are familiar to you. The government decided substantially to remove import restrictions and in other ways to pursue a firm anti-inflationary policy, and the Reserve Bank has continued with its policy of credit restraint. While there have been successive reductions in the Statutory Reserve Deposit ratio during 1960/61 they have by no means fully offset the loss of liquidity resulting from the run-down in international reserves. Banks have accordingly found it necessary to reduce their lending, and outstanding advances, as some of you will know only too well, have fallen by nearly £100m. from their peak in October 1960.

To help meet the medium- and longer-term problem the government has taken action in regard to coal-handling facilities, rail gauge standardisation, and road works in Queensland, as well as granting certain tax concessions designed to encourage the expansion of exports. Some of you might feel that these measures are inadequate; others might feel that in the name of the balance of payments we are creating anomalies which are hard to justify and at the same time are exposing sound and long-established Australian enterprises to unnecessary and unreasonable pressures.

But what would you have done? Before you decide, let me remind you that hindsight makes decisions a lot easier. And the balance of payments is one field in which we are forced to base our decisions on information which is already out of date, and where any action we take now will have little effect on imports and exports for at least months and in some instances years.

THE PROSPECTS

I will leave this thought with you while I turn quickly to our balance of payments prospects.

My comments on recent balance of payments developments so far have been related to 1960/61 as a whole. In the last few months the short-run balance of payments prospects have improved markedly. Wool prices have risen by around 15 per cent. Further wheat sales have been negotiated. Imports have begun to fall. Private capital inflow appears to have risen further. And our first-line reserves have been strengthened by the drawing of £78m. from the International Monetary Fund and the arranging of a stand-by of £45m.

But most of this improvement seems to be essentially short-term, although the improvement in wool prices and capital inflow could be continuing. It seems appropriate then that we should shift our attention from the immediate prospects to the longer-term outlook.

In the long run our export earnings must increase at least as fast as our import needs. The only ways in which we can avoid this necessity is if net capital inflow increases faster than our import needs (and I am not sure that this would be wholly desirable even if it were likely) or if net invisible payments for freight, earnings on foreign capital and so on increase more slowly than import needs, which seems unlikely.

The rate at which our import needs grow depends partly on the rate of expansion of the economy and the rate of population growth, partly on the direction of development, and partly on the relation between Australian and overseas price trends. These factors are all largely within our own control or influence, although there are some grave practical difficulties in the way of influencing them.

The growth of our export income is only partly dependent on factors and conditions within Australia. It also depends on changes in income, prices, tastes, production of competing products and so on in the rest of the world and these are completely outside our control.

It can be argued that Australia's balance of payments problems in recent years have arisen largely from our attempt to grow faster than the rest of the world's demand for our export products. Although there is plenty of room for argument about this, import needs seem to have grown at something like the same rate in volume terms as Australian output. The *volume* of exports has also grown at quite a fair rate, but the volume increases have been accompanied by deteriorating terms of trade.

As we have seen, the possible rate of growth of our imports over the long run is determined by the rate of growth of our exports. If imports tend to grow faster than exports we have to do something to slow down the one or speed up the other.

There are several technical possibilities which would slow down the growth of our import needs without interfering with the mechanism of importing or decision making. One would be to slow down our rate of growth by drastically cutting our migrant intake. Another would be by making imports dearer and we have already seen how this could be done by higher tariffs, by higher sales taxes on goods with a large import content, or by changing the exchange rate. (We should note here, however, that repeated action might be needed if the tendency for imports to grow faster than exports were a continuing one.) Another possibility would be by making goods and services with a low import content cheaper or otherwise more competitive with goods and services with a high import content. For example, a more efficient metropolitan railway system would reduce the need for a second car, and there is little doubt that the direct and indirect import content of motoring is high.

There are also several ways of speeding up the growth of our exports. Exporting could be made more profitable, by subsidies or tax concessions or by changing the exchange rate. Or the growth of 'exportable surpluses' could be speeded up by slowing down the growth of home consumption. Or the rate of investment in export industries could be speeded up in various ways.

There is not time tonight to consider further the relative merits of each of these methods. But there is one thing I want to stress—we must never lose sight of what we are trying to achieve and we must always weigh the costs of any proposal against that of the alternatives. We cannot afford to waste resources by pouring them into inefficient industries, even if they produce exports or replace imports.

I hope I have given you something to think about. If there is any conclusion it can only be this—of all the problems of an expanding economy perhaps the most difficult is the double-headed one of maintaining internal and external balance. While we seem to have gone at least some way towards solving the internal problem (and after all the solution to this is very largely in our own hands) we have been less successful in handling the external problem (which arises, at least in part, from trends and policies in other countries over which we have no control or influence). But if we cannot find consolation anywhere else we should reflect on history and realise that what today seems an intractable problem may well have been forgotten a decade hence, or have paled into insignificance beside new and more troublesome issues.

Some Ingredients for Growth

W HEN it was first proposed that I should give this address, I was deeply interested in the economic progress of several countries, particularly France and Japan, which had combined a basically free enterprise structure with a form of economic planning. My interest was particularly great because they had apparently reached a rate of growth superior to that of many other comparable countries and, indeed, to our own. Like many people, I wondered whether the techniques they employed and the results that they apparently achieved thereby were capable of transfer to our own economy.

It was clear from the published work of the planners that they proceeded by a series of approximations in the formulation of their plan, the first being a very broad picture of the economy some years ahead, built up from a number of relatively simple assumptions—the purpose being to throw up the implications of these assumptions for the basic sectors of the economy and for the main constituents of its social accounts. From then on, the practicability of the various elements in this broad picture was tested and amended in consultation with the representatives of major industrial groups, public authorities and the like until, it was hoped, what emerged was not merely something which was generally believed to be practicable but something which in the making had so moulded and influenced the attitudes and plans of the sectional interests concerned that it had become in essence a statement of intentions.

While it was clearly impossible for me to undertake so Herculean a task as the preparation of an economic plan for Australia, it seemed that it should be possible to proceed to the first stage—to prepare the first broad picture from basic assumptions and to explore its broad implications and perhaps to judge whether there was merit in proceeding to the later and more complex stages of planning.

Shann Memorial Lecture, University of Western Australia, 31 May 1963. Reproduced by permission of the University of Western Australia Press.

In the event, however, the preparation of such outlines has come to play a secondary part. In speculating about the probable growth of the economy, we can foresee roughly how the labour force is likely to grow and we know that we will be better off if this work force can be kept effectively working—that is if we can keep close to full employment. But just as important is the rate at which the productivity of the labour force can be increased and the skill and intelligence with which we deploy it; this latter is a problem of producing the right things in appropriate proportions. And so my interest has been increasingly concentrated on exploring the factors upon which growth depends and the conditions which are favourable to them—the conditions and the policies which will justify optimistic assumptions upon which to base the broad picture of our economic future.

I have prepared two sets of figures which give alternative versions of a broad picture of the economy in 1969/70. The first assumes that productivity continues to rise at about the same rate as it appears to have done over the last decade or so—by some $2\frac{1}{2}$ per cent per annum. The second alternative considers what the position would be if we could raise the rate of growth of productivity above past levels to $3\frac{1}{2}$ per cent per annum. It was hoped that these two sets of figures would give some rough measure of the benefits which could flow from such a change and that it would expose some of the major points of pressure and strain that would be entailed within the economy.

SOME MEASURES OF THE EFFECTS OF GROWTH

Before extracting a few comparisons from these figures, let me stress that the figures are not forecasts. They serve to illustrate my assumptions and to keep some check on internal consistency. If, as I hope, these assumptions are plausible, the figures help in ascertaining whether rapid rates of growth, if achieved, would create serious imbalances.

Given the maintenance of reasonably full employment, likely rates of growth in the labour force, and an increase in productivity of $3\frac{1}{2}$ per cent per annum, we could by 1969/70 increase our gross national product to £11·3 billion, compared with £6·2 billion in 1958/59 (all estimates in terms of 1958/59 prices). This amounts to a compound rate of increase of G.N.P. of 5·5 per cent per year, coming from an average increase of 1·95 per cent per year in numbers of workers and 3·5 per cent per year in productivity per worker. This compares with N.E.D.C. targets for the United Kingdom of an increase in the work force of 0·8 per cent per year and an increase in productivity per worker of 3·2 per cent per year.

On reasonable assumptions about the share of the total product going to wages and salaries, this would allow for a rise in wage and salary incomes from £3·0 billion to £5·4 billion—or an increase per head of persons employed of approximately 46 per cent. It would suggest, for instance, a rise in expenditure on beer, wine, and spirits from £277m. to £401m. and in foreign travel from £29m. to £73m.

In the public sector, it would, without fundamental changes in the severity of taxation, permit public expenditure on education, health, and social services of £1,264m., compared with £548m. in 1958/59 and expenditure on public works and development of national resources of £1,253m., compared with £575m.

A growth of productivity at 3½ per cent per annum is a very optimistic assumption but the results of growth (other things being the same) of the lower rate of 2½ per cent remain striking. It is clearly worth our while to devote some thought to identifying the main ingredients in the recipe for growth.

PRACTICABILITY OF SUCH GROWTH RATES

But before we make this identification I would like to examine briefly and, of necessity, somewhat superficially, whether growth rates as high as these are economically practicable for Australia—whether they would produce problems which without fundamental changes in social and political attitudes would be insoluble. Experience of other developing countries suggests that high rates of growth

(1) may require a rate of savings to support capital formation beyond the willingness or capacity of the community to provide;

(2) may involve an expenditure on imports which it would prove impossible to finance from export income and net inflow of capital without depletion of reserves;

(3) may require levels of taxation or public borrowing to finance government expenditure (including expenditure on public investment) which would prove to be socially intolerable or impracticable.

To decide whether the growth rates contemplated in this paper would involve such problems for Australia, answers must be provided to the questions:

(1) Given reasonable assumptions about the growth of exports and imports under conditions of rapid growth, what would be the inflow of capital required to enable us to balance our international payments?

(2) Given reasonable assumptions about the supply of business and personal savings and the inflow of capital and the demand for capital for housing, motor vehicles and other fixed investments and for stocks, what would the private sector be able to contribute by loans to government expenditure (including public investment expenditure)?

(3) Allowing for growth in public expenditures suggested by current

political and social expectations, what level of taxation would be required to balance the government's accounts?

BALANCE OF PAYMENTS

Our experience with the balance of payments will depend more on the relationship between aggregate demand and aggregate supply than on the absolute level of output. I have assumed that imports will be about the same proportion of G.N.P. as they were in recent periods of reasonable domestic balance. If productivity grows at $3\frac{1}{2}$ per cent per year this gives imports of £1,875m. in 1969/70, compared with £1,009m. in 1958/59.

Our quantity of exports has grown impressively in recent years. For many items I have assumed a continuation of trend but have been less optimistic for some categories—e.g. it seems unlikely that exports of wheat and flour could maintain recent trend rates of growth. Raw materials and foodstuffs will continue to dominate our exports and there is, I think, some reason to believe that the prices of these goods relative to the prices of our imports will follow a mild downward trend. In 1958/59 our terms of trade fell below trend and I do not think I have been over-optimistic in assuming that the trend (with which we are here concerned) will by 1969/70 have fallen to the lowest point recorded in the post-war period (a level practically as unfavourable as the worst period of the 1930s).

On this basis we would require in 1969/70 a capital inflow of about £400m. to avoid a fall in reserves. This may be a pessimistic view because I have assumed that an increased rate of domestic growth would not affect the quantity of primary products exported; the technical progress needed to achieve a growth in productivity of $3\frac{1}{2}$ per cent per year should do something to lower costs in primary industries. Four hundred million pounds is a large sum and compares with an average of about £215m. over the last four years but, when allowance is made for the growth of retained profits and the evidence of increasing European and American interest in Australia as a field for investment, is not inherently improbable. If, of course, we accepted, as perhaps we should, a greater responsibility for providing capital for countries less fully developed than ourselves, the picture could be less favourable.

PRIVATE INVESTMENT AND SAVINGS

The major uses of savings in the private sector are investment in dwellings, motor vehicles, other fixed capital (commercial and industrial buildings, plant and equipment, etc.) and stocks of goods (materials, in process and finished). The estimate of expenditure on housing substantially accepts recent estimates by Dr A. R. Hall of the number of dwellings which are likely to be needed but assumes a 0·5 per cent per annum increase in real cost, reflecting improved standards, or perhaps just increasing complexity. For cars we have assumed that with rising incomes Australia will follow the way set by the United States towards increasing the number of cars per family. I must confess I boggle at this estimate and am appalled at the thought of what the number of cars implied will do to the quality of urban and suburban life.

The provision for increased stocks of non-farm goods represents, on the basis of recent experience, 30 per cent of the projected increase in G.N.P. and at that level seems a surprisingly large share of the increase. Development in stock control depending on the use of computers has in recent years demonstrated in other countries that considerable economies are possible. This seems a fruitful field for management study. Large stocks are both expensive and wasteful and obviously if this ratio can be reduced significantly the benefits to the community of increasing productivity will be greater and more quickly realised.

Estimating the need for other fixed investment was particularly difficult since it has not proved possible to establish from past experience any plausible ratio between increased expenditure on capital and increased output. The estimate, therefore, is based on ratios of gross fixed investment expenditure (excluding housing and motor vehicles) to G.N.P. and is 0·5 per cent of G.N.P. above average experience for the last decade.

My assessment gives total demand for private investment of £2,195m., compared with £1,218m. in 1958/59. Business saving is computed on the assumption that recent behaviour concerning retention of profits by companies and allowances for depreciation will continue. With the estimated capital inflow from abroad a balance is obtained when income taxes take 10·5 per cent of personal income. This situation requires net borrowing by governments of £168m. in the year. This is not an impossible target for public borrowing.

In assessing the needs of public expenditure, resort must be had to assumptions which may prove wildly invalid, since the content and magnitude of such expenditure reflects the policies of governments and the pressures to which they are subjected. While I have tried to be influenced by trends which are already apparent in governmental budgets, there is no doubt that my own prejudices and judgments have influenced the choice of figures. Perhaps it will suffice here to say briefly that I have allowed for a more than proportionate growth in expenditure on education and health, on social service benefits, and on public works and the development of national resources.

On the revenue side, I have assumed a continuance of existing indirect and company taxes and continuance of the trend towards more frequent incorporation of business enterprises. The role of direct taxation on individuals as a balancing item has already been described.

This exercise suggests that a level of taxation would be required which in the aggregate would represent slightly more than 23 per cent of G.N.P., compared with slightly less than 22 per cent in 1958/59. However, I have provided for increases in public spending without any reductions in private propensities to spend. If there is anything in the suppositions that these propensities may be lower in the 1960s than the 1950s, we will of course be able to manage with lower levels of taxation.

The upshot of this, subject to all the uncertainties involved in the process, seems to be that a rate of growth involving an increase in productivity at an annual rate of $3\frac{1}{2}$ per cent per annum would not appear likely to involve Australia in serious balance of payments problems, would require provision of savings for private and public investment reasonably in accord with present community attitudes and could in the public sector be financed with levels of taxation not significantly different from those now current.

I must confess to some surprise at this outcome. When I commenced this exercise I expected that severe pressure on both the balance of payments and on available savings would follow from an attempt to push our rate of growth to the level contemplated by our higher example.

It is perhaps worth while looking back over this exercise to ask at what points this optimistic conclusion is most exposed. Externally the major risk is a resumption of unfavourable trends in the terms of trade. A one per cent fall in our export prices, compared with those for imports, would involve an increase in the payments deficit of about £16m.

Internally the biggest risk is probably in defence expenditure. My estimates were compiled before recent statements and reflect past trends more than recent indications of changes in policy. A rise in defence expenditures to anything like the proportion of G.N.P. devoted to this activity by our major allies would require substantial curtailment of some other expenditures and could add considerably to our bill for imports.

Both external and internal equilibria would, of course, be upset by excessive demand and it is essential that demand is not over-stimulated in attempts to attain any particular rate of growth.

MEASURES TO INCREASE PRODUCTIVITY

It is one thing to argue that a growth rate involving a $3\frac{1}{2}$ per cent per annum increase in productivity could be supported by the Australian economy but this demonstration can do little to ensure such an increase.

It is well known that increasing productivity is mainly the result of technical change—of the application of new knowledge to the products and processes of industry. Productivity will increase more rapidly only if the process of technical change can be speeded up.

For this to occur requires:

(1) a flow of new knowledge;

(2) a willingness and capacity among entrepreneurs to recognise the relevance of such knowledge and to apply it to their own industries;

(3) an industrial and commercial environment equipped with appropriate technological and financial institutions to give entrepreneurs access to capital, services, and technology required;

(4) an industrial and commercial labour force trained and adapted to technical change—at all levels from management, through technicians to skilled and unskilled labour.

RESEARCH AND DEVELOPMENT

To all of this the flow of new knowledge is basic. Contemporary experience is demonstrating the value of organised research and the costs of leaving such matters to chance. While no particular piece of research can be guaranteed to produce new knowledge and, even less, new knowledge of commercial value, there is a direct relationship between expenditure on research in the aggregate and the flow of economically valuable ideas.

Of course, the greater part of the world's research will be done outside Australia and it is important that we keep in touch with it—as indeed to some extent we do. We spend abroad some £15m. per year in payment for the use of other people's ideas—in royalties and so on. But these payments are for the *developed* ideas—for the knowledge from research applied to the products or problems of industry. Much of the research is as available to us as to those to whom we pay this £15m. and there is nothing to prevent our doing the development.

But, too, we can undertake our own research. We are all aware of the valuable work done by CSIRO, state Departments of Agriculture, and the universities in the field of primary production but few realise how much this has contributed to the growth in physical output of our export industries, which is such that our quantity of exports has grown by about 7–8 per cent per annum over the last decade.

Some exciting work (though perhaps not enough) is being done in industry in Australia. For instance, last year work done at B.H.P.'s Central Research Unit resulted in publications and patents concerning a process for continuous steel making. It has for a long time been a dream of steelmakers that a continuous process might be evolved. Work is being done towards this end in Europe and the United States. I am technically unequipped to judge whether the results of this work will stand up to the tests of commercial production. But if they do they could reduce the capital costs of establishing a steel industry and further reduce the costs of steel making. If Australia could be a 'jump ahead' in this connection, we could be in the forefront of world steel technology.

We do not lack capacity in this field of research and development but by international standards our allocation of resources to it is low. We spend approximately 0·6 per cent of our G.N.P. on research and development, which compares with expenditure in recent years, for which information is available, of 2·8 per cent in the United States, 2·5 per cent in the United Kingdom and 2·3 per cent in the Soviet Union and ranks us below such countries as Sweden, Canada, West Germany, France, Norway, and Japan.*

It could be that since our scientific resources are of necessity limited, it would be wise to concentrate more on development rather than on basic research, but here our performance seems especially disappointing. Most business enterprises consider they have done well if their technology is as up to date as their overseas principals or competitors and would regard investment in the development of a new idea, however promising, as an unwarranted gamble. For small firms this might well be true and we should perhaps consider whether our institutions are well adapted to ensuring that this function is performed.

This then is an important requirement for a higher rate of growth— a conscious effort to increase the scale and scope of research—in CSIRO and other government agencies, in universities and in large-scale businesses and to pursue more actively the application of the results of research to the practices of industry.

ENTREPRENEURSHIP

Before the knowledge which flows from research can benefit production we must have business executives who are entrepreneurs in the true sense —who have the capacity to recognise the relevance of new knowledge, to see it as an opportunity, and to bring together the capital, the skills, and the labour required to realise it. One of the disappointing things about Australia's post-war industrial development is the degree to which the entrepreneurship has been provided from abroad (and resulting profits have accrued abroad). We like to speak as if the development could not have taken place without the capital and the know-how from overseas. Some of the largest foreign owned enterprises have been built with little or no introduced capital, that is capital other than that gradually built up from undistributed profits or borrowed from Australian sources. Furthermore, the know-how is generally provided

*See S. Dedijer: 'Measuring the Growth of Science' in *Science*, 16 November 1962, p. 783.

by technicians and managers who can be hired or by patents and other process rights which can be bought. The major contribution of overseas enterprises to Australian industry may well prove to be the demonstration that entrepreneurship is practicable and that there is no reason why it should not originate here. It is partly a matter of attitude of mind —a spirit of enterprise—but more the knowledge from past experience that the diverse elements required to embody an idea in production can be brought successfully together. It is interesting to note that more recently there has been increasing evidence of entrepreneurial boldness among larger Australian companies. This has come partly by learning from example but it is backed by the consciousness of reserves of capital, skill, and organisational capacity behind them. This may well be the strongest social argument for large scale enterprises.

If this growth of an indigenous entrepreneurial spirit flourishes, then we may see a change in the character of our capital inflow—fixed interest borrowing abroad tending to replace the equity ownership now so often the standard pattern. This would be cheaper and would occasion less anxiety of the kind that is felt in Canada where so large a part of the basic resources of the country are owned and developed by foreigners.

INDUSTRIAL AND COMMERCIAL ENVIRONMENT

Effective entrepreneurship requires ready access to the various elements of production—adequate supplies of power and other public utility services, engineering facilities, insurance and similar commercial services, as well as the whole range of financial services comprehended within the banking system and capital market. Generally speaking, Australia seems well equipped with these and other institutions required to provide an industrial and commercial environment in which entrepreneurship can be effective. There do seem, however, to be certain deficiencies which are particularly relevant to the speedy application of new knowledge.

While many of the most efficient firms, particularly those with good international connections, maintain a close watch on productive techniques abroad, there is at present clearly a time lag in the application even of these techniques and little is done to watch the flow of the outcome of new research to speed its application, other than in agriculture, where the extension services of State Government departments perform well. In this connection, I have been interested in the work of the modernisation committees established as part of the French planning machinery. These committees are set up by the main sectors of French industry and serve primarily as a point of contact and collaboration with the office of the plan but, as their name implies, their function has been to ensure that the plan provides for bringing and keeping French industry in the forefront of modern technology. I wonder whether similar committees might not prove useful in Australia, not merely as a point of contact with government and other public authorities but also as a means of ensuring effective collaboration with CSIRO, universities, and other sources of new knowledge.

One of the major difficulties facing the application of research is that even a sound and potentially profitable research idea is usually quite unsuited to direct application to industry without extensive developmental work, sometimes involving further research, the production of pilot plants and adaptation to (or modification of) existing capital structures and market practices. Frequently the finance involved in these processes is considerable and some firms are too small to shoulder the risks and expenses involved. This is especially likely where the idea involves a radical departure from existing techniques and consequently involves the obsolescence of already installed capital equipment built up previously at great cost. Even though these risks are clearly significant for individual industrial projects, there is good reason to believe that, for innovation as a whole, the processes of development are profitable. There may well, therefore, be a case for establishing specialised institutions to undertake this work, either as a publicly supported service to industry or alternatively as a profit making venture financed by private enterprise itself. There are some interesting models abroad which are worth our study if we are contemplating action to fill this gap in our institutional structure.

In the United Kingdom, for instance, there is the National Research Development Corporation, wholly financed by the government. Results of research which seem to have economic importance and which originate in public research institutions, universities and the like are referred to the Corporation, which examines the possibilities of development. Its usual method is to arrange development contracts with suitable industrial firms and where it is not able to do this it makes known by a periodical bulletin to industry generally innovations and inventions which might be of interest. The Corporation has, for instance, done a great deal of work in the developing of computers, of certain medical and biological products and a number of other projects, including the hovercraft. In practice the Corporation has proved financially fairly expensive, despite the fact that it usually retains rights in the patents of its innovations, but a single major success could, of course, radically alter this picture.

An alternative or possibly a supplementary approach, which has been developed in the United States, Canada, and more recently in the United Kingdom, is the setting up of private corporations financed generally by enterprises such as banks, life assurance companies and so on, which undertake the same kind of task but essentially on a commercial basis. They choose projects which appear to offer more immediately the possibility of profit and they provide funds either by loan or, more frequently, as a share in the equity, to enterprises which are capable of fully developing the innovation concerned. The United States example, which is called the American Research and Development Corporation, is in essence an investment corporation and obtains its capital from public issues and invests in appropriate projects of this kind. It has had a remarkably favourable experience and its shareholders have been amply rewarded for their participation in this venture. A similar corporation has now been established in Canada and another on similar lines in the United Kingdom. Action on one or perhaps both of these lines may well be worth while for Australia.

Successful innovation generally depends not merely on access to capital and to ideas but most frequently to skilled personnel. The rapid industrial development of Australia during and since the last world war has produced a fairly wide spread of competent technical and administrative men in industry and commerce. It is, however, not always easy to mobilise these people for new undertakings. By contrast with the United States, for instance, there appears to be very much less movement between firms of business executives, and men in industry reach positions of responsibility and authority on the whole at a much higher age in Australia than in the United States. This reflects perhaps a more conservative attitude on the part of top management but also the fact that young Australians in industry appear less adventurous, less willing to take a personal risk by moving to a newer and more uncertain enterprise.

One factor which might stimulate such mobility of key personnel would be the development of transferability of pension rights. Private firms as well as public authorities have come to regard superannuation arrangements as a way of tying their skilled personnel to them. Such restrictive practices in the long run are rarely in the interests even of the enterprise itself. Something could no doubt be done by the negotiation of inter-company agreements on a generalised scale enabling people to move without sacrifice of superannuation privileges. The government could perhaps assist in this by allowing preferential tax treatment to superannuation arrangements which provide for transferability.

EDUCATION

Fundamentally, however, the task of producing an adequate industrial and commercial personnel, research minded, adaptable and skilled to take advantage of new knowledge, is an educational one. There is little doubt that Australia, so far from being a model in the educational field, lags badly, particularly in those aspects of education concerned with the development of this kind of personnel for industry and commerce.

Despite the fact that the proportion of G.N.P. devoted to education has more than doubled over the last decade, we still rank only fifteenth in a list of twenty-three reasonably comparable countries. On current expenditure, we devote 2·3 per cent of G.N.P., compared with 3·6 per cent in the United States, 3·5 per cent in the Netherlands, 3·2 per cent in the Soviet Union and 3·0 per cent in the United Kingdom. In total expenditure (current plus capital) we rank below Canada, Italy, Norway, Austria, France, Belgium, Denmark, Ireland, and Switzerland.*

There is no doubt that a better educated community is a more productive one and, while a generally increased investment in education is desirable, it may well be that from the point of view of stimulating productivity greater emphasis should be placed upon the technological aspects of training. There is some reason to believe that our approach to education has a clerical as opposed to a technical bias and that we have, for instance, nothing comparable with the system of polytechnics which distinguishes this aspect of education in France and other European countries. It was perhaps a pity that the one institution at university level which frankly accepted a technological bias has been converted to a university of standard model. As examination of the influence of, for instance, the Massachusetts Institute of Technology on patterns of thought in industry and in management would suggest that there would be benefits to Australia from an increase in the number and importance of technical institutions at the higher levels of education. Interesting work is being done in the United States and in the United Kingdom for the development of institutes or schools of business management within universities and other institutions of higher learning.

Indeed, there is a good deal to be said for the inter-penetration of universities and similar educational institutions into the structure of higher management in industry and commerce. I was, during a recent visit to the United States, tremendously impressed by the post-war resurgence of industry in the New England states, an area which had suffered considerable economic eclipse as a result of the movement of engineering and similar industries from that area to the middle west and the textile industries to the south of the United States. It became clear that a tremendous industrial revival had been consciously promoted by

*See P. H. Karmel, *Some Economic Aspects of Education*, Buntine Oration, Melbourne, 1962. Figures other than for Australia are quoted from I. Svennilson, F. Edding, and L. Elvin. 'Policy Conference on Economic Growth and Investment in Education', in *Targets for Education in Europe*, Washington, 1961.

interesting business in the establishment and development of industries which were research based, recognising that in the universities and research institutes of Harvard, Massachusetts, and the New England states generally there was a kind of economic resource unequalled in quality and extent probably anywhere else in the world. I have come to believe that closer relationships between university staffs and executives of industry and commerce would be mutually advantageous and that the practice of academics accepting consultations with industry could be developed in Australia.

In considering the pattern of our development for the future, we should remember that, if we lean on producing natural resources and primary products for the industrialised and industrialising countries of the world, we are relying upon commodities the demand for which will become a progressively declining proportion in the value of final products produced, and similarly that, if we rely upon the development of domestic industries dependent for ideas and technology upon other countries, we will be paying increasing tribute abroad.

We have the potential for a high degree of literacy and adaptability. Maximum development of this potential may well be the wisest investment we can make.

CAN PLANNING HELP?

This essay began as an attempt to consider the usefulness of planning to economic policy and development. It might be useful to conclude by returning to this question. It is clear that the drawing up of a plan in the sense of a model of the economy at some time in the future could serve to demonstrate how growth depends on the co-ordination of the elements of private decision-making and public policy. It could indicate the implications and possible inconsistencies of unco-ordinated sectional planning, perhaps allowing us to forecast points of pressure within the economy as a whole.

If it could achieve this purpose as a framework for more informed decision-making in the public and private sectors, it would probably justify the effort involved. But at the same time it must be realised that planning does not offer a means of escape from the problems of decision-making and the hardships of economic life. In the last resort the future of the economy must still depend on the skill and initiative of management in the public and private sectors and this can best be encouraged by sound and forward-looking economic institutions and by a highly educated and adaptable industrial and commercial community.

Maintaining
Stability in a Rapidly
Growing Economy

H ISTORIANS could no doubt find evidence of concern with growth over a very long period. But conscious concern about it as an objective of economic policy is really a phenomenon of the period following World War II. And its emergence to the forefront of such objectives contains a number of points of interest.

Initially this concern developed because economic growth, requiring as it did a high rate of investment, seemed to be the means to the achievement of full employment. The wastes and bitterness of the depression years were still fresh in the minds of many and the Keynesian revolution in economic thought offered hope of making full employment a reality largely through the maintenance of a level of investment sufficient fully to employ the potential savings of a fully employed community. The effect of such an investment program on the growth of G.N.P. and on the level of real incomes initially received little attention.

But growth quickly became the more dominant element in the credo of the advocate of progressive or active economic policies. This is perhaps not surprising. It was a more dynamic objective and expressed more adequately the demand for a better world which wartime experience made vocal. It served also as a partial reconciler of political and economic conflict inherent in the full employment objective.

For some time advocacy of full employment policies met resistance from employers and from those to whom inflation and monetary depreciation seemed the major bogeys. These could see full employment only as a condition of labour scarcity with strong trade union bargaining strength and consequently a built-in tendency towards rising costs and prices. Growth, however, to the extent it derived from greater productivity and offered a steadily expanding money demand, offered both the source from which wage earners' demands (within reason) could be met and a commercial climate favourable to enterprise and to profit making. On the other hand, it weakened the obsession of wage earners and their

Lecture to Eighteenth International Banking Summer School, Melbourne, 17 February 1965. Reproduced by permission of the Bankers' Institute of Australia.

representatives with protective 'spread the work' policies and provided a basis for their growing interest in measures designed to increase productivity.

Growth too was a more significant concept for countries with large populations and low standards of income—for most of those newly emerging from colonialism. In their countries the concept of full employment, deriving as it did from the depression experience of industrial countries, seemed irrelevant in the face of widespread poverty and under-employment both in village and city. They were concerned to break out of the vicious circle of rising population, poverty, inadequate savings, and economic stagnation. To this end growth was the only means.

It is therefore not surprising that economic growth, its sources, and its problems, have become central to the political economy, practical and theoretical, of our times.

IS GROWTH A DESTABILISER?

There is implicit in the title of this paper, and in the question to which I have been invited to direct my attention, a judgment that a high rate of growth is a cause of, or is likely to be associated with, instability. I would first like to consider whether this judgment is valid.

It is true that in most statements of the objectives of economic policy growth is linked with other targets which are concerned with stability. For example, in 1945 the Australian Government, in a paper entitled 'Full Employment in Australia', indicated the overall objectives of official policy as:

(1) full employment;
(2) stability of prices;
(3) equilibrium in the balance of payments;
(4) a rapid rate of economic development;

and I think this formulation would command fairly general support among all political groups in Australia and it would in substance be widely accepted by governments in other countries.

But I have already mentioned that a rapid rate of growth first received emphasis because it was seen as a means to full employment, that is as a means of preventing the instability of unemployment. In the same way growth, because it tends to be associated with high and rising levels of income and aggregate demand, is likely to reduce the risk of downward instability of prices arising from an insufficiency of demand. It is true that growth which derives from increasing productivity can, and in favourable circumstances does, bring about lower prices for certain classes of goods. By themselves such cost-induced price reductions are unlikely to be dramatic, especially as their associated income effects will be tending to increase demand generally. Similarly in the field of international payments growth tends to reduce the risks of certain forms of instability. During the 1930s unemployment and stagnation in the major industrial countries, accompanied by falling incomes, led directly to a decline in the demand for internationally traded goods—thus reproducing in other countries the conditions of declining demand, unemployment, and stagnation originating elsewhere. Growth, with its expansive effect on unemployment and incomes, tends to produce conditions in which effective demand for internationally traded goods is limited only by a country's capacity to produce goods and services for export or to borrow international currency from others. In this field also growth tends to reduce the risk of deflationary instability.

On the other side—in relation to the risk of upward instability, of inflationary pressure on prices and on the balance of international payments—the picture is less rosy. But even here we have already noted one stabilising influence of growth. People in contemporary society have been educated to expect an improving standard of living —by their politicians, by advertisers, by the whole impact of mass media of communication, and even by the economic statistician—who, Thomas Wilson says, 'may be the most subfuse of agitators but not for that reason the least powerful'. Such widespread expectation of improving living standards leads to continuous pressure for increasing incomes and social services which will, if the pressure is strong enough, be met in part at least in money terms. Only if these concessions are made in the context of economic growth based on rising productivity can they be given reality and their effect on pushing costs and prices upward mitigated.

Thus it can be argued that growth reduces the risks of at least some forms of instability and it may well be that an expanding economy is easier to keep reasonably stable than one in which output and incomes are static or declining. Nevertheless, experience in many parts of the world has shown that rapidly expanding economies often show the evidence of inflationary pressure on prices and frequent and persistent disequilibrium in the balance of payments.

This is not surprising. Both in countries of large population and low income and in more developed countries it is easy to see how attempts to step up the rate of growth can exercise destabilising influences. For instance, in a country of large population and low incomes measures to increase output must begin with capital formation often of the most basic kind—power, transport facilities, heavy industry and so on. In establishing these, labour is brought into employment at wage rates which are high, compared with the incomes that many of the wage

F

earners previously enjoyed, since many of them would have been under-employed in cities or villages or dependent partly on subsistence agri-culture. The consequent increase in incomes is not for some time accompanied by any significant increase in the flow of food or other consumer goods. In the absence of substantial external aid with which to finance imports the higher incomes will inevitably press on limited supplies of goods and bring about rising prices and in the international field a scarcity of international exchange.

In more highly developed countries, the demand for available sav-ings is generally at a high level already without the stimulus of special measures to promote economic growth. This demand in recent decades has been stimulated by the expansion of instalment credit which has led to a heavy demand for savings to finance consumers' capital such as housing, motor vehicles, domestic equipment and so on. Further-more, as standards expected rise, the cost of providing buildings and equipment for social services in education, health services and so on tends to rise also and to require an increasing allocation of the current flow of savings. In such circumstances any unusually large expansion of the capital formation associated with the economic growth will tend to produce claims for resources which in the aggregate will exceed what the community is voluntarily prepared to save. Unless the additional capital formation is resolutely financed in such circumstances by in-creases in taxation, upward pressure on prices usually emerges. The mechanism by which this rise emerges depends a good deal on local conditions but frequently evidence of strain is shown by labour short-ages with competition emerging between employers for scarce categories of labour and by growing bargaining strength of wage earners' repre-sentatives.

In these economies, too, pressure on the balance of international payments is likely to develop although if the structure of production is such that production for export is rising proportionately and the economy is attractive to international investment, this pressure may be mitigated.

Contemporary experience supports these conclusions. Rapidly developing countries, particularly those with low incomes per head, have almost invariably encountered inflationary pressures on their price structures and persistent difficulties in their balance of pay-ments. Despite the advantages of growth, therefore, in avoiding the risks of downward fluctuation one cannot escape the conclusion that it increases the risks of upward instability.

DOES INFLATION HELP GROWTH?

There are, of course, some who argue that this tendency for economic growth to lead to rising prices is not in itself bad, and that in moderation this particular form of instability is helpful to growth and that the injustices it involves are a low price to pay for the benefits of the growth itself. There is, of course, something in this point of view. A tendency for prices to rise brings about a redistribution of income within the community—a redistribution which tends to favour those actively engaged in the production of, or trading in, goods and services. It acts as a concealed subsidy to entrepreneurs and a concealed tax on passive savers and on those whose incomes cannot readily be adjusted to the changing level of prices. Within reason such a subsidy can have a profoundly stimulating effect. It produces optimism and confidence in the mind of entrepreneurs; it encourages them to be adventurous and provides in a sense some of the means to enable them to do this. On the other hand, however, there are serious disadvantages in using inflation deliberately as a source of the resources necessary for economic growth. Once those who have resources to lend come to expect a continuance of price inflation they will naturally seek to build into the interest rates they charge a premium to provide against the expected depreciation of the money they are lending. Furthermore, other sectors of the community—wage earners in particular—will seek to insure themselves against the effects of rising prices by various forms of built-in adjustments. To the extent that these sections of the community can insulate themselves from the effects of inflation, it ceases to have the benefits claimed for it. There is increasing pressure for inflation at a greater than the anticipated rate in order to continue to secure the bene-fits for entrepreneurs. To this process there seems no logical end short of complete destruction of the value of the currency.

Furthermore, the stimulating effects of inflation are arbitrary and uneven and do not necessarily encourage the most appropriate struc-ture of industry. In particular, we have seen already that rising domestic prices tend to be associated with difficulties in the balance of payments and yet the process of rising prices itself will tend to make concentra-tion on production for the domestic market more attractive than pro-duction for the export market. Hence the natural balance of payments difficulties associated with growth will be intensified by the distortions in the structure of industry brought about by the rising prices them-selves.

I have not touched upon the moral aspects of this issue and indeed I see no reason why a community cannot, if it wishes, choose to sub-sidise entrepreneurs if they feel this will produce economic benefit. To bring about the subsidy through inflation, however, does so with the minimum opportunity for the exercise of parliamentary or other con-trol and imposes the burden of the subsidy on the weakest members of the community. Acceptance of inflation as desirable produces too easy an answer to the budgetary problems facing governments anxious to expand their economies. It can quickly undermine financial responsibility without which a proper assessment of the social priorities among the various claims on available resources is impossible.

I would judge, therefore, that it is worth while aiming to associate stability with growth. This does not mean, of course, that a country can expect to maintain absolute stability but the fluctuations will be between fairly narrow limits and there will remain at all times an element of uncertainty about any predictions as to the direction or rate of instability.

IN WHAT CIRCUMSTANCES CAN GROWTH BE RELATIVELY STABLE?

Essentially the problem seems to be one of aiming at a rate of growth which does not bring about conflict with one of the limiting factors. Thus a high rate of growth can be achieved:

(1) when the population is growing fast or there are substantial resources of unemployed or under-employed labour or of labour engaged in industries of low productivity;

(2) when there are substantial lags in the degree to which modern knowledge and technology have been effectively applied;

(3) when there are available skilled workers, technicians, and managers to apply this knowledge and technology;

(4) when there is a high rate of savings (including a capacity and willingness to borrow and/or receive aid from abroad) or alternatively a willingness to bear heavy rates of taxation;

(5) when there exists the entrepreneurial capacity to recognise the opportunities which exist from the combination of these available resources and to apply them to socially useful purposes;

(6) when the international exchange available from reserves, from borrowing, or from current exports is adequate to maintain a balance in international payments, despite increasing imports.

It is unusual for all of these conditions to exist in favourable form in countries at the same time. It will be noticed, however, that they correspond closely to the conditions of countries of relatively high levels of productivity and income which have, because of war or other external factors, been prevented from applying their resources to economic growth for some time. It is probably because of this combination that the very dramatic rates of increase in production have been achieved in countries such as Japan and the countries of Western Europe during the last two decades.

It should be noted that the practicable rate of growth depends upon the combination of these considerations. However well endowed a country may be numerically in its labour force or in the rate at which it is growing, this will be of little value to it unless the skills, the savings, and the entrepreneurship are available. Since the training of the labour force in the appropriate skills, the development of an entrepreneurial spirit and the emergence of an appropriate structure of industry are difficult and long-term tasks, international aid providing a supplement to domestic savings and to existing international resources has in many countries proved disappointing in its effects.

CAN ANYTHING BE DONE ABOUT THESE RELATIONSHIPS?

It is important to remember: firstly that the major risk involved in a program of rapid economic growth is that this program will exert pressure on prices and the international balance; and secondly that the better the balance achieved between factors, the higher the effective rate of growth can be without this risk. While it may be difficult to establish, *a priori,* appropriate relationships between these various factors, it is almost certain that a social and economic policy can be developed which will make a significant contribution to maximising the conditions favourable to growth.

It is important to repeat that it is the combination of these factors which is important and that this in some circumstances may involve a contraction of one in order to conform more appropriately to the available levels of the others. The most obvious example of this is in relation to population. In a country of high average level of production per head and a high ratio of savings to G.N.P. a rapid growth of population can contribute substantially to economic growth. This is not necessarily true in other countries. Where the level of income and the ratio of savings are relatively low and population is rising fast, it may take a large proportion of possible savings to train and equip the increasing population at or near the existing level. This may leave little or nothing over for widening or deepening the capital structure or of raising the level of technical competence and managerial capacity. In such circumstances, if it is practicable, a limitation in the rate of growth of population may be an effective contribution to an appropriate balance in the factors contributing to growth.

It is clear that the most fundamental requirement is an effective educational policy which makes available to the work force an appropriate range of skills and knowledge and equips them to recognise and seize the opportunities which economic growth can offer. History is full of examples where social change, by opening up educational opportunities, releases a vast reservoir of human ingenuity and resourcefulness. The precise social and institutional changes which are necessary to bring about this liberation will vary from society to society since the restraints on human opportunity are infinite in their variety and can develop in societies of every institutional pattern.

The same is true of entrepreneurial capacity. It is clear, from our own history and that of other peoples opening up the new world, that individual access to the means of production proved in the circumstances of that time tremendously liberating and creative. Subsequent history suggests that changing technology and the increasing complexity of economic production now places a much greater emphasis on corporate activity. The way in which entrepreneurial capacity is best recognised and given opportunity in corporate organisations is a question about which it is difficult to generalise but the continued success of corporate economic organisations may well turn more on their capacity to recognise and to give opportunity to the man of entrepreneurial spirit than on the precise political, economic, or commercial principles on which the corporation is constructed.

Just as the organisation of economic production tends to become more collective in character so too does the economic function of savings. In all forms of society we rely more upon the institutions which mobilise savings and those, including governments and their agencies, which save on behalf of the individuals. In societies which are basically capitalist in their structure we rely increasingly on life assurance, superannuation funds, private and public corporations and on the government itself to impose and mobilise the savings of the community. In collectivist economies the emphasis is even more heavily on the role of the government as the instrument and mobiliser of savings. In newly emerging communities the establishment of appropriate institutions for the encouragement and mobilisation of individual savings and for encouraging private and public corporations to perfom this role effectively can be developed by public policies. There is no doubt that the effective operation of such institutions can, by raising the proportion of income which by savings is available for capital formation, lift the sights of economic growth some notches higher.

Restrictions on growth imposed by shortages of international exchange are difficult to overcome effectively by domestic action. Something can be done no doubt in the planning of development to concentrate on activities which will produce goods for the export market. It cannot be too strongly emphasised that production for exports gives command over goods and services in general and consequently provides a vital element of elasticity in the working out of economic growth. However, it is here that international action can be most effective. The more developed countries of the world can, by providing access to their own resources and skills, by loans or aid in the form of foreign exchange, do much to make more effective domestic policies directed to this end.

However, when the most that is practicable has been done to create conditions favouring economic growth, it will remain necessary to accept a rate of growth which is consistent with limits set by the balance that it has been possible to achieve. Furthermore, it will be necessary to watch and to recognise the symptoms of a rate of growth which presses unduly strongly against these limits and having recognised them to be willing to accept some restraint.

Capital, Growth, and International Payments

I WANT to start by saying a little about what I understand by capital, which in physical terms we tend to think of as durable equipment used in the production of future goods and services. Thus, factories, plant, and equipment, as well as farm improvements, roads, power plants, administrative offices, shops, are all characteristic forms of capital. But the concept also covers other things to which we have devoted our resources which are capable of increasing future production or consumption. It includes, for instance, consumers' capital, such as houses, hospitals, libraries, art centres, and opera houses but also productive capital embodied in the skill and knowledge which comes from education and training; in new knowledge and technology which comes from research and development; and most generally, in the improvement of the physical, intellectual, cultural and social environment in which we live, the quality of which affects profoundly the character of our lives. Let us not forget that this, after all, is the final purpose of all economic activity—to enable people to live better. Where we devote current production to producing durable goods, facilities or amenities of the kind I have described, we are producing capital, and resources for their production must be provided from our own savings or from the savings of other people.

OUR CAPACITY TO ADD TO CAPITAL

Having said that to show what I mean by capital, let us go on to look at capital in Australia. No one has usefully estimated the total quantity of capital in use in Australia or its distribution between various industries. We can do a little better in estimating the amounts of new capital formed year by year. Thus it has been estimated that over the last five years we have spent $27\frac{1}{2}$ per cent of our income or G.N.P. on capital goods. That $27\frac{1}{2}$ per cent would not include all the kinds of expenditure that I have referred to a moment or so ago. It would not, for in-

Address to the Australian Industries Development Association, Melbourne, 26 September 1967. Reproduced by permission of the Reserve Bank of Australia.

stance, include expenditure on the development of new knowledge or new technology.

However, even allowing for the exclusion of those items, this 27½ per cent is a very high figure, comparing favourably with most countries in the world, although it does fall short of what is achieved by Japan, which has, I think, the highest ratio of investment to G.N.P. or of new capital formation to G.N.P. in the world.

Now this high level of new capital formation reflects itself in Australia—and indeed in Japan too—in a very high growth rate. Figures that were issued along with the last budget estimate that the value of our production in recent years, excluding variations in prices, has grown at a very steady rate of about 6 per cent annually, except for the drought year of 1965/66. With population growth of about 2 per cent a year, we have raised output per head by more than 3½ per cent per year, even allowing for the effects of the drought. Now, by anybody's standards, that is a very impressive performance; but I do want to look at the questions of whether we could have done better and, incidentally, whether it would have been worth while.

Capital formation has to be financed. It has to be financed by saving, by somebody setting aside some part of his income and not spending it on current consumption. Now the savings necessary to finance this new capital formation have been provided in Australia in the following ways: governments and public authorities have accounted for about 6 per cent of G.N.P. (6 per cent out of the 27½ per cent). The private sector, including businesses as well as individuals, have provided 18½ per cent and the rest of the world—the people who have lent us money or invested it here—have provided 3 per cent.

If we are going to look at whether we could have done better in our achievement, the first thing we have to decide is whether we could have increased that 27½ per cent to a higher figure and then, of course, to see whether we could have made effective use of a higher figure or whether we could have made better use of the figure we now have. Having a look first at the question of whether we could have increased that 27½ per cent, let us look first at governments and public authorities. Now, they could have increased their contribution to savings only by imposing higher taxes and charges or, on the other hand, by reducing their current outlays. I think there are few people who would advocate higher taxes, even for so economically virtuous a purpose as a higher growth rate and, while I am sceptical about claims that are often made that taxes have reached their upper limit, I think it is realistic to agree that increases in taxation would to some extent at any rate be offset by a reduction in private savings. So, there does not seem to be much to be hoped for from an increase in saving by the public sector on that side of their balance sheet.

On the side of expenditure, of course, there are plenty of people who see all forms of public expenditure as inherently extravagant and a proper subject for the pruning knife. I do not entirely share these views, although I would not deny that there is some waste in public expenditure—probably much about the same percentage as there is in private expenditure. On the other hand, as incomes and standards of living rise, more of the goods which can add appreciably to the quality of life are characteristically provided collectively and it is increasingly necessary to take collective action to conserve and improve our physical environment. A well-planned town or city, with uncluttered roadways and an effective transport system, which is rich in parks and gardens, has fine buildings, libraries, art galleries, theatres and the like, with easy access to areas of unspoilt rural and natural environments, is the foundation of a good life for the citizen and it becomes increasingly difficult to preserve and more expensive to create. And only public authorities can do a great many of these things, so that for these reasons we should not hope for much increase in savings by a contraction of public expenditure.

There is, however, one form of public expenditure which is encroaching seriously on our provision for growth. This is expenditure on defence and war. Now I am not competent to judge the urgency of the need for this expenditure or the wisdom of the way in which it is spent. I think it is sufficient to say that expenditure on defence and war is a cost that we will pay for by having to accept a slower rate of growth than would otherwise be possible. I think it is possible to say further that the lower we can keep—consistent with safety—our expenditure on defence, the more quickly we will be able to grow and, looking ahead, the easier it will be to provide whatever is necessary in the way of defence goods and services. However, that takes me well beyond the scope of my present subject.

Let us turn now to look at the possibilities of increasing private saving. Whether you can do anything about private saving by policy action is extremely uncertain. Certainly our experience shows that it helps if there is a wide range of securities available to meet the taste and convenience of savers of all kinds. Our experience shows also that reasonable stability of prices strengthens the incentive to save, especially if this reasonable stability is strengthened from time to time by periods where prices do not rise at all (this is necessary to confound those characters who bet on prices always rising). If we have these conditions of reasonable stability, it is clear that this does give savers confidence and they are more likely to be prepared to set aside current income for the benefit of the future. But no one wants to save from income now if he knows that when he wants to use these savings at some future time they are going to be worth substantially less than now. Nothing is a bigger incentive to spending quickly than a feeling that your money will rapidly depreciate the longer you leave it unspent.

Much is claimed from time to time about special concessions in the tax structure to favour those who save. Indeed, some concessions of this kind are built into our own tax law. It is hard, however, to see much benefit in a concession which is confined to a particular form of saving—it may affect merely the composition of saving and if at the same time it reduces revenue and consequently public saving, we may be the worse off for that particular concession.

However, I think there is a different story about tax concessions that apply to all forms of saving. Some years ago I suggested that thought might be given to financing the desired level of capital formation by a special form of income tax which would give a rebate for all income saved, assessing the amount saved by the increase, for persons and for companies, in their net worth over the year. I still find this idea attractive, although tax administrators blench at the thought of its complexity and some financial writers saw in it a 'socialistic' device; though I may say, recalling my friend Mr John Dedman, that I can think of nothing more likely to encourage lower income people into becoming 'little capitalists'.

However, if we could achieve an even higher level of domestic savings than the 24½ per cent we have achieved over the last five years, there would undoubtedly be promising benefits. We may well be able to sustain a higher rate of growth and with a higher rate of growth a more rapidly increasing level of income and improving standards. Apart from this—and I know this is of interest to businessmen—economically life is simpler when the economy is growing fast. Business expectations are more readily fulfilled and, even if they happen to have been rather extravagantly calculated, in due course growth will catch up with them. Furthermore, since most of you have to meet the persistent desire of wage earners to share in what they see as the steady upward growth in production, the fact of growth makes it a little easier to meet the demands that they put upon you. Consequently, there is a good deal to be said for growth.

Furthermore, we could ourselves own a larger proportion of these capital assets created if we ourselves saved more. We would need to borrow less from abroad, or, alternatively, if we were content to go on borrowing from abroad, we could perhaps ease the restraint that the wicked Reserve Bank places upon your freedom to invest outside Australia. This would aid development in neighbouring countries and perhaps open new opportunities for Australian enterprise. So the benefits from a higher rate of savings are considerable.

On the other hand, we do have to remember that if we do save more it becomes the more urgent that we have capital expenditure projects on which to use the savings. For if we fail to have those capital projects we may once again face unemployment and waste of resources. Now, of course, it seems to me—as I hope it does to you—ridiculous to suggest that in Australia we may lack profitable and useful projects on which to spend our resources. At the same time, I have been a little worried over the last year at the persistent slowness of private investment spending to pick up from a slightly low level it reached a year or so ago. This suggests that businessmen may need to be a little more flexible and perhaps more adventurous in the search for new projects. However, on the whole I would not rate the danger of our not being able to use increased savings resources as very serious.

Finally, of course, there is a point beyond which it is not good sense to sacrifice present consumption to the future. If I may make an illustration here—the recent somewhat disturbing reports of more widely spread poverty among the old and the sick in Victoria than most of us would have been prepared to admit existed does suggest perhaps that there are some claims on our current resources that should have some priority even over those needed for growth.

Let me turn to that part of our savings which we get from outside Australia. This is a little more than 10 per cent of the total—3 per cent out of 27½ per cent of G.N.P. But this amount, small though it is as a proportion of the total, may well be the margin which lifts us into the high growth rate league and, therefore, it is important to Australia. Now, it is well known, of course, that there is some anxiety about our dependence on this inflow of capital from outside Australia and I would like to touch on some of the questions that can reasonably be asked about it.

First of all, looking at it from the point of view of Australia as a whole, is it good business to borrow so much? Secondly, are we building up economic risks for the future by this borrowing? And, thirdly, are we establishing dangerous enclaves of foreign ownership in our industries?

Looking at the first of these questions and assuming we are, as I have argued and believe strongly, a good growth prospect, it seems to me to be good business to borrow, even though we have a high rate of domestic savings ourselves and even if we could raise it further. Given growth, it will be easier to repay from a higher G.N.P. in the future than to cut our consumption further now. We have borrowed pretty heavily in recent years yet the cost of servicing this borrowing abroad—as measured by the rent, interest, and dividends accruing abroad each year—has remained remarkably stable at about 2·1 per cent of G.N.P.

On the whole, it does not seem to me that there is any risk at the moment of this not being good business. As to risks, capital inflow is uncertain being, as we have learned during the last two years, influenced by public policies as well as by economic conditions in the countries from which it comes, and therefore subject to some extent to unpredictable changes. A combination of adverse influences on capital inflow with bad seasons and poor export prices could, without doubt, face Australia with a painful adjustment similar in kind to that which hit us back in the late 1920s. However, we are less exposed now than we were then. Our exports are more varied and represent a much smaller proportion of our G.N.P. Our reserves are reasonably healthy and are buttressed by international institutions designed to help us and others meet just such contingencies. Clearly, therefore, I would say the risks of allowing capital inflow or borrowing abroad are well worth while taking. But nevertheless they are real risks and their existence emphasises the need for good reserves and for a high rate of domestic savings.

Turning to the question of the distribution of foreign capital and its concentration on some areas in the economy, it can fairly be said that the distribution of foreign capital through the economy in Australia is uneven. To some extent this reflects certain features in our own institutions and capital markets. The capital market and our system of public finance have tended to concentrate the use of domestic savings in certain fields. We finance almost entirely the public investment program of governments and semi-governmental bodies. We finance almost entirely the construction of houses; we finance almost entirely the provision of transport facilities. Again, we finance almost wholly expenditure on farm improvement and other rural investment and, generally speaking, we finance in the main smaller-scale manufacturing enterprises.

There has therefore been a tendency for large-scale enterprise—particularly in mining and large-scale manufacturing—to be the special preserve or special area of influence of foreign capital. Now I see nothing particularly harmful in this concentration. These are industries in the main where we probably have most to gain in access to know-how in large-scale operation. But it is a pity if it happens merely because of organisational weaknesses in our capital market or in a lack of entrepreneurship on the grand scale in our industrial community.

There are, however, growing evidences that Australians are learning quickly to mobilise resources in large-scale ventures and innovations in our capital market are increasingly enabling it to cope with very large raisings. Here, if I may be permitted to say so, I have a confident hope that the newly established Australian Resources Development Bank will play an important part in increasing our capacity to give effect to this mobilisation.

But the diversion of Australian savings into large and exciting ventures does not, let me remind you, necessarily increase the total of such savings and if we put more of our savings into big ventures we may well have to turn to other sources for a greater part of the savings needed for other forms of capital formation. In this respect, the easiest but obvious suggestion to make is that governments could borrow more of their requirements abroad and, so far as this can be done without impairing the markets for the governments themselves, it could be helpful for us to diversify our overseas borrowing a little. It is hoped, for instance, that the Australian Resources Development Bank will itself be a borrower abroad for short- and medium-term funds in amounts and from sources on the whole unlikely to be tapped by governmental issues.

There have, too, been some interesting experiments which suggest that housing may be a possible avenue for the use of overseas savings. There are some institutional problems associated with this development but I see no reason why they should be insuperable. Interesting also are the movements of foreign capital to agricultural and pastoral developments. These are interesting not merely because it is a relatively new development of scale but also because it might provide a demonstration to our own large-scale entrepreneurs that here are fields of development which can yield handsome returns to those prepared to spend substantially and wisely and who are able and prepared to wait for a few years for a return.

On the whole then I think the case for continued encouragement and welcome to foreign investment is pretty well established for our circumstances. But, as I say, I do not think we should sit down and leave exclusive areas to overseas people—exclusive to them not for any technological or efficiency reason but from a failure on our part to modify our own institutions and to be really genuinely enterprising. If we fail in these two respects, we should not be captious about the help which we derive from overseas capital.

COULD WE USE OUR SAVINGS MORE WISELY?

Could we have done better with the savings that we have or could we do better with an increased volume of savings? Here I am concerned not with the amounts but with the use that is made of them. Now it may seem captious even to raise this question, as I began by saying that our performance both in the amount of savings and the resultant rate of growth was very creditable by any international standard, but it is the function of an economist (and I used to be one) to seek to make the best use of limited resources.

Many questions could be asked on this topic of whether we use our resources wisely, but I want to confine myself to three which seem to me to be fairly important. The first is: would we do better if we accepted a somewhat smaller population growth? Secondly, are we wasting resources by unwise development, particularly where it is encouraged by the use of protective devices? Thirdly, are we neglecting the opportunities for investment in that form of capital I referred to in new knowledge and new skills?

Looking first at the question of population, we have population growth of about 2 per cent per annum and this means that a substantial part of our savings is necessarily used to equip the newcomers at the exisiting standards—every new family needs a home, access to schools, to hospitals, a place for the breadwinner to work, a piece of a farm, a factory, a shop, or an office or what have you. Clearly, if our population growth was somewhat smaller, if in effect we had slightly fewer migrants, theoretically at any rate we would be able to equip a smaller work force more adequately than we can at present and it would be a reasonable assumption that, better equipped, they could increase their output per head more rapidly.

This, of course, is not solely an economic question. Along with most Australians I regard immigration as a 'Good Thing'. It has brought very welcome diversity to our population and has enriched our community with skills and talents we can properly value.

Despite the cost in reduced equipment per head, I am inclined to think it worth while also from a strictly economic point of view. We have the physical resources for large-scale production but we lack in important fields the sound base of a mass home market. A rapidly growing population is both a strong stimulus to investment and to enterprise and an insurance against the effects of excessive optimism. In a world of shifting technology and changing demands, it enables us to redistribute our resources, particularly our labour, with a minimum of social friction.

Consequently, I would conclude that the benefits of a reasonably rapid population growth outweigh for Australia the costs of spreading our capital formation a little more thinly over the population.

However, I myself would argue that we are fairly close to the optimum of our present rate of population growth—certainly in the years when we attempted a migration flow which brought the annual increase in population to something over 2½ per cent there were abundant evidences of strain in the economy.

Turning to the question of development sponsored by protective policies: over the years I think the policy of protecting industries capable of development has, despite occasional extravagances, served us well. It has enabled us to bring into production resources which might otherwise have long lain idle. It has enabled us to build up in a skilled labour force, in supervisory and managerial capacity, in a wide range of financial, industrial, and technical services available to industry, in a growing cadre of skilled and experienced entrepreneurs, an industrial environment which did not exist before, in which the real productive capacity of this country can be developed on a competitive basis. Its effects are reflected in the wide range of industries producing for consumers (we now spend only about 2 per cent of our gross national product on imports of finished consumer goods) and also it is evident in the many industries which are demonstrating in export markets their capacity to compete with the world on equal terms.

But I think the time has come when we can, with advantage, review the generality of this policy of protection and begin to use it with more discrimination—remembering at all times that when the economy is fully employed, and this is the prevailing condition of our economy, a subsidy or a tariff in one area of industry reduces spending power or raises costs in another. I think you will agree one needs a good reason to penalise one industry for the benefit of another.

Conditions are now substantially different from the time when this widely protective policy was adopted. So long as we continue to be a good growth prospect there is little doubt of our capacity to achieve substantial full employment. Secondly, we were able in those days to carry through an extensive policy of protection because its burden fell primarily on export industries of a large-scale agricultural and pastoral type whose output, so far from being restricted by the higher costs, was, in some circumstances at least, stimulated into more economical methods—the more easily since for most of the time they were working on a substantial profit margin. Today the most important of these industries may well be struggling for survival. Furthermore, the make-up of our exports is increasingly shifting to minerals, meat, wheat and, most interestingly, to manufactures, the rise of which in our export figures over the last five years has been most dramatic. Now in some of these industries marginal additions to costs can be critical. We have shown that there is a wide range of industry within which we can produce and sell competitively with the world and there is much to be said for concentration of our resources to a greater extent in these industries.

Now an additional reason, I believe, exists in the changing structure of world trade. Increasingly the industries of the newly emerging countries of Asia are knocking at the door of the markets of the world. These countries—not far away geographically from this country —are in many cases our present markets and, even more importantly, our future markets. Our prosperity over the coming decades is likely to be as much bound up with the success they have in raising their standards of production and income as it has been bound up over the last twenty years in the great growth of Japan. It is very much in our interests that the great markets of the world—in the United States and in Europe—should open their doors to the products of these countries and enable them to raise their standards of income and of living. Consequently it is very much in our interests that we set a good example to the rest of the world.

Some of the protection given here arises from a desire to provide a base for large-scale production in industries offering substantial economies of scale. I have sometimes wondered whether the device of some limited pooling of markets between countries is not a device worth fighting for. We would have to fight to be able to achieve it, in the face of resistance from established industrial powers—in the commercial councils of the world. A kind of common market between a regional group of countries, covering only particular industries, might well provide the opportunity—much more cheaply than extreme protectionist devices—of giving economies of scale to industries while still preserving something of a competitive environment. It is hard to see why a common market covering everything is virtuous, and a common market covering only a limited number of commodities is sinful. I think this is an idea which it would be worth while industries and government exploring.

Above all, is it wise to continue to use protective devices for maintaining producers in industries where it has been proven over the years that they lack the requisite resources or capacity? Let us indeed protect them against short-term fluctuations, let us be generous and humane in helping them into other occupations but surely it is foolish to burden the other industries in our economy with the relics and mistakes of the past. Such policies are no kindness to those concerned in these industries, who face in any case a declining future, and it is, believe me, an injustice to their children.

Briefly, on this question, I would say:

(1) We are a good growth prospect and resources, particularly capital and entrepreneurial skill, will, for many years, continue to be scarce in this country. We should therefore economise in using them where they can be best employed.

(2) More and more of our industries will for effective operation depend less on local consumption and more on exports and on the production of capital goods.

(3) It will pay us to concentrate on these with an eye to economies of scale and not to burden costs by attempting to do a little of everything.

(4) We stand to gain by international commercial policies which give the newer and poorer countries of the world a chance to raise their standards of income.

Now let me emphasise this is not a case for no protection but an argument for a more discriminating use of it.

CAPITAL IN THE FORM OF KNOWLEDGE

Finally, I want to turn to the question of whether we have devoted enough of our capital, enough of our savings, to that form of capital which is embodied in knowledge. Increasingly industry becomes more and more dependent on human skills and knowledge—skills embodied in highly trained and experienced workers, technicians, scientists, technologists, supervisors, managers and entrepreneurs—and knowledge embodied in processes and in know-how. These resources do not come into the world unbidden or by accident. They must be planned for, worked for, and paid for.

In the past we have largely been content to borrow or to buy other people's knowledge. Now within limits this is good sense and good business—the world has built up and is adding, year by year, to a vast store of knowledge and skill, which we would be short-sighted to ignore and, judging by the cost of payments for patents, royalties and the like which we pay out overseas each year, I think we get good value for what we spend. However, to rely solely on the results of other people's work in these fields is to condemn ourselves to industrial mediocrity.

A few years ago I criticised Australian industry in this respect— saying that with a few honourable exceptions Australian enterprises were content to accept the best overseas techniques as the best possible. Since then the honourable exceptions have become more common but the interaction between newly emerging research and technological development and Australian industrial practice is still far from impressive by international standards.

Let me quote three examples from overseas. I am told that if a Japanese firm finds it necessary to install an imported machine, machine tool, or even a whole plant, there descends upon it before and during installation, and in the early stages of operation, a team of perhaps twenty young engineers, each of whom will write a personal report for the management on the equipment and its possible improvement. Often before it is even installed they have proved it to be obsolete or at least obsolescent. But where do you think the next machine, machine tool or plant is constructed; and who enters the international market for the supply of such equipment?

In the State of Massachusetts, U.S.A., there is a whole range of industries which has grown there because in and around the city of Boston there is the greatest concentration of universities and research institutes in the world. There is a constant and planned communication between top management and technicians in industry and the scientists and teachers in the universities and institutes. These industries, chemicals, pharmaceuticals, electronics and the like—the science based industries—lead the world in their fields. And they lead the field because they make use of a particular resource that they have in that area—the existence of scientific knowledge and scientifically trained people.

In America and in Europe it is standard practice for major firms to engage university teachers and research workers as part-time consultants. In Australia communication between universities and research institutes on the one hand and industry on the other is surprisingly small. There is a vast storehouse of stimulus and ideas exisiting in this country largely neglected by industry.

Accordingly, I commend the recent action by the Australian Academy of Science in setting up a Science and Industry Forum to stimulate the interchange of ideas between industry and science but this Forum is not likely to get far unless there is a change of heart on the part of much of Australian industry.

Now I make this point for a particular reason. We in Australia are passing through a phase of unprecedented discovery of natural resources. Over the last few years we have discovered bauxite, iron ore, nickel, natural gas, oil, and copper in great quantities, actual and potential, and these are by no means the end of it. At the moment our activities in these fields are largely exploitative, directed to export markets in relatively unprocessed form. Everybody expects, however, that in due course these resources will become the basis of a highly sophisticated processing and manufacturing industry, with a great variety of associated enterprises. But it must be recognised that it may be decades before this development can be fully achieved.

Now what an opportunity is there here? Are we going to sit back and accept, at each stage of the development of these industries, the best available technology from overseas? Or are we going now to devote real resources to the problems of these industries so that when we come to the next stage of development we will be in the forefront of technology, not just in the ruck? In some of these industries technology is already in a state of flux and change is inevitable and, about the rest, who knows what intelligence, energy, and resources will reveal? It seems to me that here a planned assault on the science and technology of these future industries by a partnership of the firms concerned—Australian Government research enterprises, universities, and institutes of technology—would be a splendid adventure and would almost certainly pay handsome dividends to the owners of these developing industries.

In other words, I am convinced that in the long run the most important capital for industry is the capital which is embodied in knowledge and in the people who possess it. One of my fellow bankers has a slogan which urges you to 'Get with the Strength'. My advice is 'Get with the Knowledge'. Cast your bread generously on the waters in this respect and it will almost certainly return to you many-fold—and in the meantime, it will open up for you new horizons more exciting than any you have known.

Training for Development

T HAT this is the 'key note' address for your Technical Training Year suggests that it should be devoted to telling you you cannot get very far with development unless your technical training marches with—or preferably ahead of—your development program. However, that you have had the wisdom to plan a Technical Training Year at all, that you are launching your new Institute of Technology, that you are bringing together men and women of many nations to share their knowledge and experience, and that your program of study and discussion almost overwhelms me by its scope and diversity, all suggests that I would be preaching to the converted—a dull exercise for preacher and congregation. I propose, therefore, to seize this opportunity to strike a few notes which, so far from being 'key' notes, may provoke some initial discord. The efforts to resolve such discords may provide some fun for those engaged and may even increase their understanding of the nature of the system of harmony they are hoping to build.

THE RIGHT ROAD

But have no doubt—you are on the right road. The only economies whose development is not restricted by shortages of trained personnel are those which have not yet broken out of the vicious circle of poverty, shortage of capital, and stagnation, or those which have become stagnant from the failure of the entrepreneurial spirit.

In all those underdeveloped countries, which in the last few decades have been trying to raise their productivity and incomes, the lack of trained and competent manpower—artisans, technicians, managers, administrators—has proved a more serious limiting factor to development even than the lack of capital. It is possible for an underdeveloped country to borrow capital or to receive it as grant-in-aid and in this way

Opening Oration, Technical Training Year in Western Australia, Perth, 16 March 1966. Reproduced by permission of the Western Australian Chamber of Manufactures.

to get access to the physical resources—materials, equipment and the like—of the world at large. To some extent, of course, such borrowings or aid give access also to the human resources of other countries but here many more difficulties are encountered. Human beings cannot be hired and moved as freely or as cheaply as material goods and even where they can be persuaded to do so, the application of their skills in the new location involves special problems. A technology, particularly in its human aspects, cannot simply be imported—it must be adapted to the new environment in which it is to function—and this adaptation depends upon the presence of a complex of related skills. The most difficult task facing a country wishing to industrialise itself is to build the supply of persons and institutions which service industry in its technical operations, the existence of which a firm in an established industrial environment can take for granted. There is then no substitute for the building up, early in the stages of development, of the basic structure of technical education.

FIRST STAGES

In the first stages the task of technical education, whether in schools or within the enterprise itself, is to import and adapt a technology already in use and to produce the persons equipped to employ it. As progress along the road to economic development is made, it becomes evident that increasing emphasis must be placed upon modifying the old and creating new technology to meet the needs of domestic industry. The resources of all countries differ in availability and in cost and even for the same or a substantially similar product the technology will differ from country to country if it is to make the best use of its special advantages and aptitudes.

At an even later stage it becomes apparent that the existence of highly skilled personnel in all phases of industry and in the development of technology becomes a significant factor in planning and shaping the pattern of future development.

PATTERN THROUGH DECISION

Some years ago I was greatly struck by the way in which the present pattern of industry in the New England states of the United States had come into being as the result of conscious decision. These states, though wealthy in capital, were earlier in the century facing decline following the movement of industry—engineering westward to Chicago and textiles south to sources of cheaper power and raw materials. It was realised that the New England states were uniquely rich in the supply of universities, institutes of research and technology and possessed a population of a high degree of literacy and technical competence. Consequently, efforts were made to attract to the area and to establish there industries which were dependent for their growth on just these factors—industries which were based on the results of recent research, calling for a high level of intelligence and training and capable of rapid and progressive adjustment to change. The area has now become the centre of the electronics, chemical, and other similar industries. These two processes have tended to support each other and the concentration of institutes of research, technology and higher training in the area has been intensified.

Thus, as the standard of economic achievement rises, the role of technical education becomes less imitative and increasingly positive and creative. Accordingly, it is not surprising that comparisons between countries at different stages of development or between different periods of growth of the same country establish a close connection between the degree of development and outlay on the development of and the training for technology. These items of outlay rise not merely absolutely with increasing income, but also as a proportion of total production and of physical capital formation. Modern firms pay as much, if not more, attention to the recruitment of skills and talent as to the search for capital. Indeed, J. K. Galbraith says that any successful firm, provided it performs the appropriate rites, can obtain capital but it has to work to recruit its talent. Thus he says a good firm will send its 'most imposing' man to the bank or the money market but its most eloquent and persuasive to the schools and colleges in search of talent.

From the point of view of the individual, the influence of training on earnings is usually one which makes training a profitable investment. In particular cases earnings are affected by tradition, monopolistic practices, and so on, but in the large there is no doubt that the better trained are the better paid and that, conversely, the unskilled form an increasing proportion of those who lose jobs.

There is then an overwhelming case in favour of generosity, both private and public, in the development and support of technical education—a fact which I hope will be not merely a source of comfort to the educator but also a weapon in his eternal battle with financial authority. Technical education is a good investment and an increase in the resources available to it is likely to give a greater return in the progress of development than a corresponding increase in expenditure on say, the production of capital equipment.

HISTORICAL HANDICAPS

Technical education in British communities has suffered in the past from a number of handicaps which have led it to be regarded as the poor relation of the more honoured literary and scientific disciplines.

Firstly, it evolved from and has been largely identified with the teaching of traditional crafts and occupations which remained substantially unchanged, sometimes for centuries. This has adversely affected its pedagogy, which often was hide-bound and unimaginative and unaffected by new developments in other parts of the educational structure. It has also made it difficult to adapt its curriculum and the scope of its work to the rapidly changing needs of industry in periods of technological innovation.

Secondly, it has been isolated from the creative and growing phases of industry and technology. Research has tended to be the function of the university, the specialised research institute, or the firm itself. The process of development which follows from the emergence from research of new knowledge or new processes has tended to by-pass instruments of technical education and to be taken up directly by industry itself.

Thus, those engaged in training for a rapidly evolving technology have been isolated from the stimulus and excitement which comes from contact with its growing points. Their minds have not been directly stimulated by the work of scientists and research workers or their practicality sharpened by functional contact with higher management.

Thirdly, it has been widely believed that an education with technical or professional foundation provides a less liberal or culturally rich experience for the young than those based on the so called liberal arts. As a result it has tended, with the exception of unusually clear sighted or dedicated characters, not to attract as high a proportion of either teachers or scholars of outstanding merit as other branches of education. This is not true of other countries. In Europe, and in particular in France, the polytechnics are recognised not merely as providing the highest level of professional and technical training and status but also as the source of a general education as culturally rich as that of the colleges and universities. The difference between them is one of specialisation and emphasis rather than of quality and standing in the community.

ANSWERS

I would like to say a little about each of these handicaps since I believe that if technical education is to contribute fully to development they must be broken down.

Institutions of technical education have, of course, already done much to break down their identification with traditional and unchanging crafts. An ever-increasing diversity of courses related to the newer technology is presented and teaching methods and equipment are developing fast. No doubt the main obstacles are inadequacy of resources and the conservatism of public and politicians. However, education will need to think positively to reduce the proportion of its training which is specific to particular methods of work and to increase attention to principles in order to make their trainees more adaptable and capable of meeting the needs of technology subject to rapid change. It will need also to go beyond the schoolroom to factory boardroom or union meeting to break down the prejudice and fears which limit acceptance of new methods. It will need also to bring within the range of its pedagogy the skills of management and even of entrepreneurship itself.

MANAGEMENT LAG

Too much, in Australia particularly, has skill in management had to be learned by trial and error. Despite honourable exceptions, management capacity in most Australian industry lags far behind the best in the world. We can no longer afford amateurs in management. This stricture applies, too, to the quality of directorship in the boardroom. The record of many Australian companies in recent years has led some authorities to question whether their directors understood the functions and responsibilities of a director or knew how to go about giving effect to them. This would not be surprising—there is an almost complete absence of facilities by which one entering on these responsibilities can acquire the rudiments of his profession or gain access to the accumulated experience of others.

It may be that great entrepreneurs must be born rather than made; the capacity to recognise an opportunity and to have the ability to mobilise the resources and the skills necessary to take advantage of it is obviously to some extent dependent on native wit. On the other hand, recent experience suggests that most entrepreneurship is now exercised by large and well-established companies, which suggests that the qualities it calls for can be institutionalised and, therefore, learnt. There is a fruitful source of inquiry here.

NEED FOR RESEARCH

I believe it to be of paramount importance that the isolation of the technical educator should be broken down. Just as research is a fundamental part of the functions of a university, so too it must become of a technological institute. The influence of this research must be made to pervade the whole of the technical structure. There must be movement of staff within the structure so that all may be aware of and stimulated by it. Only so can students at lower levels experience the excitement which this work brings and recognise the discipline and integrity it imposes. As students pass from the schools and institutes of the system they should take with them into industry an awareness that technology is not a body of knowledge and of techniques but a process—indeed almost a way of life. Many years ago Bernard Bavink, in his standard work on *The Anatomy of Modern Science*, wrote: 'Technology is not . . . merely applied science but is a cultural field for itself standing on an equality with art, science, and ethics as the fourth realm of values'. While there may be danger in endowing technology with too great dignity as an end in itself rather than as a means, there is no doubt that a greatly increased awareness of the potential and demands of technology can add much to the efficiency and stature of those directing our productive processes.

The entry of the institute of technology into research need not be seen as an intrusion into the field of, or unnecessary competition with, universities. Some overlap is probably unavoidable and may well be fruitful but there is a natural division of labour which will protect against undue duplication and waste. Fundamental research for which universities are best fitted tends still to be carried out with a bias towards individual rather than group work and within the limits of the academic discipline professed. Increasingly, problems of research emerge from the practical problems of industry which calls for team work crossing the border of particular disciplines. Such problems may well be better tackled within the technological institute whose practices will already encourage such joint effort.

Similarly, research which is directed to the solution of specific practical problems—so called 'applied' research—tends to be of this kind. These problems emerge characteristically at the 'development' stage —the stage of seeking to realise in production the possibilities created by the results of fundamental research. They are technological in character, they are 'interdisciplinary' in their form, and they often imply opportunities or problems in the field of technical skills. They fit naturally into the field of work of the technological institute.

The effectiveness of applied research will depend in part on effective communication within industry itself. From industry will come some of the problems to which such research is directed and it will be in industry mainly that the results of 'developmental' research will be applied. It is important, therefore, that there should be the flow of men and ideas between industry and technical tertiary education. Only if managers and proprietors are research minded and recognise that a firm or industry or an economy which does no more than borrow its technique from others, must soon languish in the doldrums of inefficiency will the best return be obtained from our investment in technical development and training. And it is on management that it will be necessary to rely for knowledge of the way in which changing technology is varying the pattern of skills which they will need to employ.

RESEARCH INTO TECHNOLOGY

Could I at this stage plead for the inclusion in your plans for the development of research in the technological field, provision for some study of the effects of changing technology itself. I believe that developing technology can ease the burdens and enrich the content of human life and few would deny this. The technological ideal of seeking to ensure that whatever is made is fitted to its purpose as well as human ingenuity and wisdom can assure is, too, one which lends purpose and dignity to its efforts. But one does not need to reject these propositions or to become one of those pessimists who sees technology only as a threat to civilisation—a dehumanising influence, destructive of moral and æsthetic values—to be aware that technological change has frequently had effects beyond the area to which the test of 'fitness to purpose' has been applied and that these effects can in some cases be seriously deleterious to human welfare. Just because we believe in the virtues of technology and because it is part of our function to promote its development and to train our young people to use and profit from it, we should be prepared to see it in a human context and pay some attention to the influence it will have on the quality of life and the environment within which it is lived.

The fundamental pattern of human experience upon which man's happiness and dignity depends is surprisingly simple and surprisingly unchanged by the physical and social differences between one environment and another. Given the means to keep alive, activities justified by a sense of purpose, and the means to cultivate the basic personal relationships, human life can be satisfying, dignified, indeed noble, at all stages of technological development. No one would, I think, question that there have been some aspects of technological change which, however much they may have contributed to the field of material production to which they relate, have endangered to a greater or less extent the opportunity of men and women to life of such qualities.

TECHNOLOGY AS AN AID TO LIVING

There is, I believe, the need for a study which might be called the Ecology of Urban Industrial Man, whose purpose would be to study the relationship between man and his material and social environment as it is being or is likely to be affected by technological change. Such questions, for instance, as the effect of certain insecticides (which form a beneficial element in agricultural processes), the effect of certain detergents and wastes on urban water supplies, the effect of universal individual motor transport on the viability of cities are at present the subject of violent prejudice or at best partial and imperfect analysis.

Human ecology would at the least help us keep cities livable as they grow—help guard against multiplying opportunities for interfering with one's neighbours' welfare—and at best might provide a rationale for positive development of the human environment and an enrichment of the relationships between it and those who live in it. I myself believe that we may, in the more developed countries, be approaching a stage where more can be achieved by such conscious modification of the environment than by the further proliferation of goods in the market place.

We should, therefore, aim at a system of technical education which is as diverse and comprehensive as technology itself, which is equipped to explore and to innovate, as well as to preserve and instruct; which provides a high road of communication between the techniques and processes of production and the fountain of advancing knowledge; which recognises its potential for and its responsibility to the quality of life within the society it serves.

TECHNOLOGY AND CULTURE

Finally, let me touch on the belief that an education with a technical or professional foundation provides necessarily a poorer cultural experience than that based on the liberal arts or sciences. This is the kind of belief which, once accepted, tends to prove itself. An education so valued will be relatively starved of resources and will, except for the dedicated, often attract less of the available talent. These deficiencies will intensify its under-valuation.

Fundamentally the belief is based on a kind of snobbishness. John Dewey observed that it reflected 'a political theory which saw human beings as permanently divided into those capable of a life of reason and those capable only of desire and work'.

Some years ago, in speaking to graduands of the University of Western Australia, I said, 'Any discipline can be the starting point for an education which is culturally rich, provided its formal content is regarded as a starting point and not as an end and provided that the scholar is in one way or another brought into contact with the developing fringes of his subject'. It seems even more appropriate that I should repeat these words here.

I believe a technical education system integrated and imbued with the spirit of innovation in the way I have advocated would be capable of providing such a culturally rich experience. It requires, of course, that its educators recognise that their purpose is not merely to produce craftsmen, technicians, technologists, and the like but men and women equipped not merely to promote and service the productive processes of the economy but also to accept their share of responsibility in the conduct of our society and equipped to enjoy in all its richness the life which opens before them. There is every reason to believe that, given the resources and the confidence of their community, our technical educators will respond to the challenge. May this Technical Training Year be the start of a new era for them.

PREPARING FOR
RETIREMENT

P REPARATION for retirement is a subject about which I know next to nothing and, while people—including myself—talk much more freely about matters of which they know nothing, I am still reluctant to undertake this task. However, I detected in your Chairman's invitation a hint that perhaps time was running out for me, too, and that I should be thinking about this matter on my own account—and there is truth in that. Accordingly, these are the rambling preliminary thoughts of a man considering his own problem of retirement for the first time.

People who are facing the prospect of retirement appear to have a collection of fears about the future. They fear the effects of loss of income; they fear the loss of the status which went with the particular role they have been playing; they fear the loss of the activities which formed so large a part of their lives and which may leave a gap difficult, if not impossible, to fill. They fear also the loss of sense of purpose; that suddenly the justification of their life will be cut away. They fear the loss of the companionship of the people who have been engaged in the same work. Naturally they fear, too, the probability of ill-health and the consciousness that death is not so far away.

I have tried to think a little about each of these fears and to wonder how I myself will face them. It is in relation to the problem of loss of income that you are likely to be most disappointed in me. I am a banker and perhaps you imagine that I will be able to produce some magic financial formula to defeat this loss of income. I must quote my wife, who assures me that my knowledge of financial matters is strictly theoretical. However, for most people the loss of income associated with retirement is relative and if one is lucky it can coincide with a reduction of responsibilities. By this time, children are grown up and educated and the withdrawal from more active life allows one to escape some financial obligations. Furthermore, of course, the Tax

---

Address to the Old People's Welfare Council of Victoria, Melbourne, 21 August 1963.

Commissioner takes a good deal more from those with high incomes than from those with low, so that the net loss after taxation is not quite as bad as it may have looked beforehand. Nevertheless, a change in the pattern of life is necessary if the new pattern is to be accommodated comfortably within the reduced income. Clearly this adaptation must take effect not suddenly on the day of retirement but be planned for over years. One must start to simplify one's life much earlier than the retirement date.

We have built up in our contemporary way of life an unnecessary complexity. Peoples in many parts of the world live with dignity and comfort on incomes that to us would appear appallingly low. With thought, we can simplify our own personal lives so that they can be encompassed with dignity and relative financial ease on lower incomes.

Here I would like to lead on to the next loss: the loss of status. Some elements in our way of life are often imposed on us, not by necessity or by taste, but by a desire for status. We must differentiate between things which are really significant and those which seem important only because they confer status. True status is a matter of personal dignity. This is an internal quality and the need for it is satisfied by a consciousness of being a worthwhile person with worthwhile functions in society and has little or nothing to do with the quality of the clothing one wears, the kind of car one rides in, or any of the things which are associated with status in the affluent society.

Indeed, some of the most interesting people I have encountered establish their own status symbols of quite different kinds. For instance, one—a director of the Bank of England—is known all through London because he rides a pushbike from his flat in the West End to the Bank of England, where he parks it among the Rolls Royces of the other directors. For him this pushbike is a status symbol—perhaps of a rather inverted kind.

I remember, too, Professor Giblin of the University of Melbourne, whom some of you may have known—one of our most distinguished economists. He was known amongst his friends and colleagues and by the newsboys of Melbourne by his shabby homespun suit and the narrow strip of red ribbon he wore as a tie. These marked him out all his life, from when he was an undergraduate, and they served him as a status symbol of a personal and individual kind. Clearly, men and women of individuality and character make their own symbols and in doing so shed the burdens which conventional society would place upon them.

The next danger—that of the loss of sense of purpose—is much more fundamental. It is a danger to which those in an absorbing occupation are especially faced at the end of their careers. The ultimate danger of retirement and old age is boredom. The morning when you wake and say to yourself 'What on earth can I do today?' you have reached the danger point.

Self respect demands that one's existence is justified by performance, at least to oneself. This is perhaps a puritanical thought. We don't ask the flower that grows by the wayside what its purpose is; it is enough in itself. Few of us would go as far as Bernard Shaw, who argued that every person should appear at reasonable intervals before a qualified jury to justify his existence, which should be summarily terminated if he failed to do so. This is extreme and I often wonder what would have been Bernard Shaw's own fate at certain times in his life if he had had to face such a jury.

However, we are most of us puritans to some extent and therefore a sense of purpose is a requisite of a happy retirement. We must, I believe, seek it in the activities with which we fill our retirement, because it is in those that purpose can be expressed. It is most effectively expressed when it lies outside yourself, when the focal point of one's activities is beyond one's own immediate satisfaction. This is difficult for those whose lives have been occupied with their professional or personal careers. A set of activities capable of occupying your time, absorbing your interest and providing sufficient stimulus can be effectively built only if the building begins a considerable time before retirement.

Of course, there are limits to what one can fairly do to prepare the way. I played golf the other day with a man about to retire and, as we were coming up to the eighteenth fairway, he said: 'I have just had a solemn thought—from next week I will have to play golf in my own time'. I remember driving to work one morning fairly early and seeing standing by the wayside a retired man, who had not been noted during his official career for early arrival at work or for any great display of energy. But there he was, bright and early, so I stopped and picked him up. I remarked as we drove along that he was going to town somewhat early for a retired man. 'Oh well', he said, 'it's different now. Now I am working for myself.'

While I would not recommend these before-retirement procedures, one should take time to develop interests and activities other than those connected with the job. There is, of course, an infinite variety of occupations and interests that can be pursued by older people. I would not presume to tell others how they should go about choosing them, but there are certain principles which I would keep in mind. The activities should be worthwhile in themselves, not merely because they help to solve a personal problem but because in their own substance and content they are exciting. In this way one's attention is directed outwards. As one grows older personal, physical, mental, and spiritual problems become more obsessive. It is important to break the tendency to self-centredness which is perhaps especially strong in people as they get older. Secondly, the activities should be balanced so that they exercise all aspects of one's being. They should give physical activity; they should stimulate and exert the mind; and, what is frequently forgotten, they should excite the emotions.

I would like to elaborate a little on these three aspects. Bodily activity is the means to pleasure in physical existence. This is why games are so popular and important. It is good that old people should go on playing games. I intend to play golf until I cannot play any longer. Then I shall play bowls until that, too, is beyond me. Then, I hope, I will play marbles or something else. Not merely do games give pleasure in muscular exertion and the pleasant weariness of extended effort but also because in them even the most pedestrian of us achieves occasionally moments of perfection—an aesthetic experience rare for most people in other aspects of life. There is a tendency, because the body becomes tired more readily and recovers more slowly, to play games or to work in the garden less frequently. This, I think, is wrong. It is better to be active more frequently, but perhaps for not so long at one time. More frequent activity keeps capacity alive.

Physical activity is the easiest objective for Australians. They are by tradition players of games and it is easy for people in retirement to continue. But in the intellectual field the effort is greater. But here, too, exercise is essential to our capacity to understand and appreciate. It is not sufficient to read the same books, to look at the same pictures, to listen to the same music. We must continue to experiment and to learn—to learn a new language or to acquire a new skill can be an exciting experience. Not long ago, as a kind of therapeutic exercise, I took to oil painting. I found this enormous fun; not merely were the physical processes pleasant and the results exciting (if not always satisfying), but I found through it a new way of looking at the world. As you walk through the gardens you will suddenly see a stone, a tree, or a flower not just as a visual or æsthetic experience, but as a subject matter for paint. This is a completely different vision; suddenly the whole conceptual universe is fresh and new.

In intellectual things, therefore, do not accept the pattern of present mental life, but try new things. It is one of the weaknesses of old people to be suspicious of the new. This needs to be resisted. Not, of course, that all new things are good or better—but we cannot really judge their relative merits until we give them a go.

The conviction that emotional exercise is a requirement of a full life is even less appreciated, even by younger Australians. Emotions do need exercise—in fact, an active emotional life may well be essential to complete health. I don't comprehend the biology of these matters, but I believe that the fluids secreted into the bloodstream when emotions are active are a stimulus to vitality. The Greeks argued that one should participate in ceremonies and theatrical performances so that vicariously one could experience the emotions of pity and terror. I think they were right. Other emotions, too—the emotions of tenderness, compassion and, on occasions, anger and indignation when these are called for, should not be restrained. The full richness and quality of personal life can be lost if emotions are perpetually suppressed, or if occasions likely to evoke them are avoided.

La Rochefoucauld remarked that the passions of youth are no greater enemy to happiness than the apathy of old age. Let us remember that youth has no monopoly of emotional life, and let us seek opportunities to stimulate our own.

There are many wrongs in the world to be righted; there are many weak and unhappy people to be protected and comforted. To work for a cause is to give your emotions not merely the opportunity to become conscious but to be effective in action. Some people find this stimulus and experience in religion, where the sense of identity with the forces behind the universe can enrich their emotional lives. Like the Greeks, we, too, can get vicarious experience from art, music, and the theatre. But friendship and love for other men and women are the easiest and the richest source of emotional wealth.

In all of these things—activities of the body, mind and of the emotions—there is need for balance. The great oriental religions and philosophies make great play of the contrast between activity and contemplation and in many of their exercises, physical and spiritual, they seek to balance one against the other. This, too, one can deliberately plan; to find not merely those activities which are lively but those which encourage reflection and contemplation.

All this suggestion of planning a nicely balanced range of activities and interests rather suggests that one would on retirement lead a sort of time-table life; that one would have one's week scheduled out to provide for them all. This is not what I intended, but there is something to be said for the idea. As I mentioned earlier, the worst thing that can happen is to wake in the morning and wonder what on earth you can do. It is not a bad idea, therefore, to wake and say: 'Today I must do this and that and so and so—this is on the program'. Such regularity gives life a rhythmic ritual quality which is satisfying to the human spirit. Of course, you may be one who feels that escape from the tyranny of a time-table is the great attraction of retirement. But I remember G. K. Chesterton saying once that a heretic needs an orthodoxy, because you can't be a heretic except against an orthodoxy. So if you are the kind of person who likes to rebel against time-tables, it may be useful to have a time-table against which to rebel.

A balanced set of activities provides also a way of solving the worst problem of retirement, that is the danger of loneliness. Companionship in a job is rather a special kind of companionship, because it tends to be non-emotional. It is sometimes good to have people with whom one has only working relationships, in whom one's emotions are not much involved—indeed there are times when one escapes to such people with something of a sense of relief. But if on retirement you have a variety of activities, if you play golf, if you belong to a club of painters, or work for a charitable cause, there will be others engaged there with you. It is surprising how pleasant it is to work or play with other people, even when you know that in more intimate relationships you would find them intolerable. For this type of companionship a shared activity is essential. But for the richer rewards of friendship or of love one must be prepared to work. One of the great deficiencies of contemporary life is the decline of real friendships. Many people come to retirement with only the friends they made while they were still at school. Since leaving school their personal relationships have been only of a business kind and when the business basis has gone the relationship has ended. Friendships must be cultivated and the art is complex but rewarding. Do not forget how important at this, as at other ages, is friendship and love between men and women. Everybody knows they are important, but they are often thought to be the privilege of the young. This should be disputed.

Recently I read an amusing rhyme:

King David and King Solomon led merry, merry lives,
With many, many lady friends and many, many wives,
But when old age crept over them, with many, many qualms
King Solomon wrote the Proverbs and King David wrote the Psalms.

Perhaps some of the Proverbs would not have been so bitter if Solomon had saved up some of those early love affairs for later! Certainly the capacity of men and women to give delight to one another is not confined to the young. I had the good fortune to realise this when at about eighteen I fell in love with Nora O'Connell, who at that time was approaching retirement and who died not long after. She was what my irreverent sons would call an 'old bag', and I can't call her to mind in a physical sense very clearly. I remember very vividly, however, her wonderful Irish voice that would as easily woo you into a state of dog-like acquiescence or flay you with the knife edge of excoriating wrath. She was an exciting person and a delight to be with and it made me realise so early that feminine charm had no age limit and that it was not only of Cleopatra that Shakespeare said, 'Age cannot wither her nor custom stale her infinite variety'. For me still—and I hope to the day I die—women are exciting; old ones as well as young. In this I am sure there is great happiness and content.

To try to sum up what I have been trying to say—my youngsters say to me 'Dad, be your age'. This is good advice, but it's hard to know what one's age is. It has been said that a man knows his age and a woman computes hers. This is evidence of the superior wisdom of women. Age is not merely a matter of chronology and one should seek to know objectively one's age in the real sense. Then it is wise to live within limits appropriate to that age, but not to be afraid to stretch them to their utmost capacity.

Ultimately, of course, one must become conscious that death is near. I like the story of H. G. Wells who, when he was being given a dinner on his seventieth birthday, said that, when he was a child and his mother or nurse called to tell him it was time for bed, he always protested. His protest, he recalled, lacked conviction because by then weariness was upon him and he knew his time had come and that, indeed, bed would be welcome. So, he hoped, would this be true of the final sleep.

INDEX

Arbitration, 123-4
Asian markets, 168-9
Australian Resources Development Bank, 71-2, 165-6

Balance of payments, 12, 14, 27, 29, 53, 98, 103-6, 129-37, 140, 141, 143, 153, 155, 156, 157
Bank of England, 2, 15, 58
Banking, 3, 13, 16-26 *passim*, 33-4, 37, 38, 40, 47, 50-1, 63, 64, 66, 67-8, 71, 72-4; in New Guinea, 75-83, 86-91
Banking legislation, 17, 22, 47-8, 49; commercial, 71
Bills, Treasury, 13, 14, 15, 23, 29-30, 36, 38
Budgetary policy, 14, 30, 42, 114
Budgets, 62, 66, 127, 142, 155
Building societies, 68-9
Business entrepreneurs, 144, 145-6, 148, 155, 156, 157-8, 177

Capital, definition of, 160
Capital formation, 161, 163, 164-6 *passim*
Capital market, 45, 46, 47-51, 52-6, 64-5, 71, 114, 122, 137, 140, 158, 165
Central Bank, 11, 14, 15, 16, 17, 19, 22-5 *passim*, 30-1, 33-9 *passim*, 42, 45, 57-63, 119, 135
Central Bank legislation, 60-1, 74
Commonwealth Bank, 14, 15, 16, 28
Commonwealth government, 13, 23, 46, 58-63 *passim*, 134, 152
Commonwealth Sinking Fund, 14
Consumer credit, 47, 51-2
Consumer spending, 28, 39, 46, 51-2, 100, 103, 110, 125-6, 142
Cost of living, 101-2, 103, 106, 116, 117, 118, 151

Defence expenditure, 143, 162

Deposits, 11, 18, 19, 38, 41, 47, 48, 70, 71, 131, 135
Devaluation, 133
Development, 28, 54, 71-2, 97-115, 119, 120, 126, 127, 144-8 *passim*, 165-8 *passim*, 170, 173-81; in New Guinea, 76-7, 78-81, 85, 86, 87-8, 91-2

Economic fluctuations, 9, 11, 12, 13, 15, 19, 21, 25, 27, 28, 33, 38, 42, 43, 51-2, 53, 54, 132, 154, 155, 165
Economic measures, 11, 28, 30, 33, 41-3, 65, 70, 98, 99, 106, 132-3, 134
Education, 148-50; technical, 174-7, 180-1
Employment, 9, 12, 14, 24, 26, 29, 32, 51, 52, 62, 101, 119, 124, 139, 151, 152, 156
Environmental improvements, 119, 128, 163, 179-80
Exchange rate policy, 131, 132, 133, 137
Exports, 19, 27, 28, 33, 100, 102-5 *passim*, 112, 120, 127-37 *passim*, 140, 141, 144, 156, 158, 165, 168

Finance companies, 66-8, 73
Fiscal policy, 14, 27, 30, 54, 62, 143
Foreign banks, 72-3
Foreign capital, *see* Overseas capital and investment

GNP, 108-9, 139, 141, 142, 143, 145, 149, 151, 157, 160, 161, 164, 168
Galbraith, J. K., 175
Government expenditure, 13, 23, 29, 45-6, 100, 102, 127, 128, 140, 161, 165
Government finance, 69-71
Growth, 138-50, 151-9, 160-72

Hire purchase finance, 28, 39-40, 41, 42, 46, 47, 49, 51-2, 66, 100, 110

Designed by Cathy Ackroyd
Set 10 point Times, two point leaded, and printed on 94 gsm Printspeed,
by Gillingham Printers Pty Ltd
106 Currie Street, Adelaide, South Australia